12 Sermons
on Commitment

Charles H. Spurgeon

Baker Books

A Division of Baker Book House Co.
Grand Rapids, Michigan 49516

CONTENTS

Paperback edition issued 1978 by Baker Books
a division of Baker Book House Company
P.O. Box 6287, Grand Rapids, MI 49516-6287

Formerly published under the title
Twelve Sermons on Obedience

ISBN: 0-8010-8137-8

Sixth printing, September 1995

Printed in the United States of America

God in the Covenant

"I will be their God."—Jeremiah xxxi. 33.

WHAT a glorious covenant the second covenant is! Well might it be called "a better covenant, which was established upon better promises." Heb. viii. 6. It is so glorious that the very thought of it is enough to overwhelm the soul, when it discerns the amazing condescension and infinite love of God, in having framed a covenant for such unworthy creatures, for such glorious purposes, with such disinterested motives. It is better than the other covenant, the covenant of works, which was made with Adam; or that covenant which is said to have been made with Israel, on the day when they came out of Egypt. It is better, for it is founded upon a *better principle*. The old covenant was founded on the principle of merit; it was, " Serve God and thou shalt be rewarded for it; if thou walkest perfectly in the fear of the Lord, God will walk well towards thee, and all the blessings of Mount Gerizim shall come upon thee, and thou shalt be exceedingly blessed in this world, and the world which is to come." But that covenant fell to the ground, because, although it was just that man should be rewarded for his good works,'or punished for his evil ones, yet man being sure to sin, and since the fall infallibly tending towards iniquity, the covenant was not suitable for his happiness, nor could it promote his eternal welfare. But the new covenant, is not founded on works at all, it is a covenant of pure unmingled grace; you may read it from its first word to its last, and there is not a solitary syllable as to anything to be done by us. The whole covenant is a covenant, not so much between man and his Maker, as between Jehovah and man's representative, the Lord Jesus Christ. The human side of the covenant has been already fulfilled by Jesus, and there remains nothing now but the covenant of giving, not the covenant of requirements. The whole covenant with regard to us, the people of God, now stands thus: " I will give this, I will bestow that; I will fulfil this promise; I will grant that favour." But there is nothing for us to do; he will work all our works in us; and the very graces that are sometimes represented as being stipulations of the covenant, are promised to us. He gives us faith; he promises to give us the law in our inward parts, and to write it on our hearts. It is a glorious covenant, I say, because it is founded on simple mercy and unmixed grace; quite irrespective of creature-doings, or anything that is to be performed by man; and hence this covenant surpasses the other in *stability*. Where there is anything of man, there is

5

always a degree of mutability; where you have anything to do with creatures, there you have something to do with change; for creatures, and change, and uncertainty always go together. But since this new covenant hath now nothing whatever to do with the creature, so far as the creature has to do anything, but only so far as he is to receive: the idea of change is utterly and entirely gone. It is God's covenant, and therefore it is an unchanging covenant. If there be something which I am to do in the covenant, then is the covenant insecure; and although happy as Adam, I may yet become miserable as Satan. But if the covenant be all on God's part, then if my name be in that covenant, my soul is as secure as if I were now walking the golden streets; and if any blessing be in the covenant, I am as certain to receive that blessing as if I already grasped it in my hands; for the promise of God is sure to be followed by fulfilment; the promise never faileth; it always bringeth with it the whole of that which it is intended to convey, and the moment I receive it by faith, I am sure of the blessing itself. Oh! how infinitely superior is this covenant to the other in its manifest security! It is beyond the risk or hazard of the least uncertainty.

But I have been thinking for the last two or three days, that the covenant of grace excels the other covenant most marvellously in the *mighty blessings* which it confers. What does the covenant of grace convey? I had thought this morning of preaching a sermon upon "The covenant of grace; what are the blessings it gives to God's children?" But when I began to think of it, there was so much in the covenant, that if I had only read a catalogue of the great and glorious blessings, wrapped up within its folds, I should have needed to occupy nearly the whole of the day in making a few simple observations upon each of them. Consider the great things God has given in the covenant. He sums them up by saying he hath given "all things." He has given you eternal life in Christ Jesus; yea, he has given Christ Jesus to be yours; he has made Christ heir of all things, and he has made you joint-heir with him; and hence he has given you everything. Were I to sum up that mighty mass of unutterable treasure which God has conveyed to every elect soul by that glorious covenant, time would fail me. I therefore commence with one great blessing conveyed to us by the covenant, and then on other Sabbaths I will, by Divine permission, consider separately, one by one, sundry other things which the covenant conveys.

We commence then by the first thing, which is enough to startle us by its immense value; in fact, unless it had been written in God's Word, we never could have dreamed that such a blessing could have been ours. God himself, by the covenant, becomes the believer's own portion and inheritance. "I will be their God."

And now we shall begin with this subject in this way. We shall show you first that this is a *special blessing*. God is the special possession of the elect, whose names are in the covenant. Secondly, for a moment or two we shall speak of this as being an *exceedingly precious blessing*, "I will be their God." Thirdly, we shall dwell upon *the security of this blessing*, "I *will* be their God." And fourthly we shall endeavour to stir you up to *make good use of this blessing*, so freely and liberally conveyed to you by the eternal covenant of grace; "I will be their God."

Stop just one moment and think it over before we start. In the covenant of grace God himself conveys himself to you and becomes yours. Understand it: *God*—all that is meant by that word—eternity, infinity, omnipotence, omniscience, perfect justice, infallible rectitude, immutable love—all that is meant by God—Creator, Guardian, Preserver, Governor, Judge,—all that that great word "GOD" can mean, all of goodness and of love, all of bounty and of grace—all that, this covenant gives you, to be your absolute property as much as anything you can call your own: "I will be their God." We say, pause over that thought. If I should not preach at all, there is enough in that, if opened up and applied by the all-glorious Spirit, to excite your joy during the whole of the Sabbath-day. "I will be their God."

> "My God!—how cheerful is the sound!
> How pleasant to repeat!
> Well may that heart with pleasure bound,
> Where God hath fixed his seat."

I. How is God especially the God of his own children? For God is the God of all men, of all creatures; he is the God of the worm, of the flying eagle, of the star, and of the cloud; he is God everywhere. How then is he more my God and your God than he is God of all created things? We answer, that in some things God is the God of all his creatures; but even there, there is a special relationship existing between himself and his chosen creatures, whom he has loved with an everlasting love. And in the next place, there are certain relationships in which God does not exist towards the rest of his creatures, but only towards his own children.

I. First then, God is the God of all his creatures, seeing that *he has the right to decree* to do with them as he pleases. He is the Creator of us all: he is the potter, and hath power over the clay, to make of the same lump, one vessel to honor and another to dishonor. However men may sin against God, he is still their God in that sense—that their destiny is immovably in his hand; that he can do with them exactly as he chooses; however they may resent his will, or spurn his good pleasure, yet he can make the wrath of man to praise him, and the remainder of that wrath he can restrain. He is the God of all creatures, absolutely so in the matter of predestination, seeing that he is their Creator, and has an absolute right to do with them as he wills. But here again he has a special regard to his children, and he is *their* God even in that sense; for to them, while he exercises the same sovereignty, he exercises it in the way of grace and grace only. He makes them the vessels of mercy, who shall be to his honor for ever; he chooses them out of the ruins of the fall, and makes them heirs of everlasting life, while he suffers the rest of the world to continue in sin, and to consummate their guilt by well-deserved punishment, and thus, while his relationship is the same, so far as his sovereignty is concerned and his right of decree, there is something special in its loving aspect towards his people; and in that sense he is *their* God.

Again: he is the God of all his creatures, in the sense that *he has a right to command obedience of all.* He is the God of every man that was ever born into this earth, in the sense that they are bound to obey him. God can command the homage of all his creatures, because he is their Creator, Governor, and Preserver; and all men are, by the fact of their creation, so placed in subjection to him, that they cannot escape the obligation of submission to his laws. But even here there is something special in regard to the child of God. Though God is the ruler of all men, yet his rule is special towards his children; for he lays aside the sword of his rulership, and in his hand he grasps the rod for his child, not the sword of punitive vengeance. While he gives the world a law upon stone, he gives to his child a law in his heart. God is my governor and yours, but if you are unregenerate, he is your governor in a different sense from what he is mine. He has ten times as much claim to my obedience as he has to yours. Seeing that he has done more for me, I am bound to do more for him; seeing that he has loved me more, I am bound to love him more. But should I disobey, the vengeance on my head shall not fall so heavily as on yours.

if you are out of Christ; for that vengeance incurred by me has already fallen upon Christ, my substitute, and only the chastisement shall remain for me; so that there again you see where the relationship to all men is universal, there is something special in it in reference to God's children.

Again: God has a universal power over all his creatures *in the character of a Judge.* He will "judge the world in righteousness *and his people with equity.*" He will judge all men with equity it is true; but, as if his people were not of the world, it is added afterwards, "his people with equity." God is the God of all creatures, we repeat, in the sense that he is their Judge; he will summon them all before his bar, and condemn or acquit them all, but even there, there is something peculiar with regard to his children, for to them the condemnation sentence shall never come, but only the acquittal. While he is Judge of all, he especially is *their* judge; because he is the judge whom they love to reverence, the judge whom they long to approach, because they know his lips will confirm that which their hearts have already felt—the sentence of their full acquittal through the merits of their glorious Saviour. Our loving God is the Judge who shall acquit our souls, and in that respect we can say he is *our* God. So, then, whether as Sovereign, or as Governor enforcing law, or as Judge punishing sin; although God is in some sense the God of all men, yet in this matter there is something special towards his people, so that they can say, "He is our God, even in those relationships."

2. But now, beloved, there are points to which the rest of God's creatures cannot come; and here the great pith of the matter lies; here the very soul of this glorious promise dwells. God is our God in a sense, with which the unregenerate, the unconverted, the unholy, can have no acquaintance, in which they have no share whatever. We have just considered other points with regard to what God is to man generally; let us now consider what he is to us, as he is to none other.

First then, God is my God, seeing that he is *the God of my election.* If I be his child, then has he loved me from before all worlds, and his infinite mind has been exercised with plans for my salvation. If he be my God, he has seen me when I have wandered far from him, and when I have rebelled, his mind has determined when I shall be arrested—when I shall be turned from the error of my ways. He has been providing for me the means of grace, he has applied those means of grace in due time, but his everlasting purpose has been the basis and the foundation of it all; and thus he is my God, as he is the God of none else beside his own children. My glorious, gracious God in eternal election; for he thought of me and chose me from before the foundation of the world, that I should be without blame before him in love. Looking back, then, I see election's God, and election's God is my God if I be in election. But if I fear not God, neither regard him, then he is another man's God and not mine. If I have no claim and participation in election, then I am compelled to look upon him as being in that sense the God of a great body of men whom he has chosen, but not my God. If I can look back and see my name in life's fair book set down, then indeed he is my God in election.

Furthermore, the Christian can call God his God, from the fact of his *justification.* A sinner can call God—God, but he must always put in an adjective, and speak of God as an angry God, an incensed God, or an offended God. But the Christian can say, "my God," without putting in any adjective except it be a sweet one wherewithal to extol him; for now we who were sometime afar off are made nigh by the blood of Christ; we who were enemies to God by wicked works are his friends; and looking up to him, we can say, "my God;" for he is my friend, and I am his friend. Enoch could say, "my God," for he walked with him. Adam could not say, "my God," when he hid himself beneath the trees of the garden. So that while I, a sinner, run from God, I cannot call him mine; but when I have peace with God, and am brought nigh to him, then indeed is he my God and my friend.

Again: he is the believer's God by *adoption,* and in that the sinner hath no part. I have heard people represent God as the Father of the whole universe. It surprises me that any reader of the Bible should so talk. Paul once quoted a heathen poet, who said that we are his offspring; and it is true in some sense that we are, as having been created by him. But in the high sense in which the term "childhood" is used in the Scripture to express the holy relationship of a regenerate child towards his Father, in that sense none can say, "Our father," but those who have the "Abba Father" printed on their hearts by the spirit of adoption. Well, by the

8

spirit of adoption, God becomes my God, as he is not the God of others. The Christian has a special claim to God, because God is his Father, as he is not the Father of any else save his brethren. Ay, beloved, these three things are quite enough to show you, that God is in a special sense the God of his own people; but I must leave that to your own thoughts, which will suggest twenty different ways in which God is specially the God of his own children, morethan he is of the rest of his creatures. " God," say the wicked; but " *my* God," say God's children. If then God be so specially your God, let your clothing be according to your feeding. Be clothed with the sun; put on the Lord Jesus. The king's daughter is (and so let all the king's sons be) all glorious within; let their clothing be of wrought gold. Be clothed with humility, put on love, bowels of compassion, gentleness, meekness; put on the garments of salvation. Let your company and converse be according to your clothing. Live amongst the excellent, amongst the generation of the just; get you up to the general assembly and church of the first-born, to that innumerable company of angels, and the spirits of the just men made perfect. Live in the courts of the great King; behold his face, wait at his throne, bear his name, shew forth his virtues, set forth his praises, advance his honour, uphold his interest; let vile persons and vile ways be contemned in your eyes: be of more noble spirits than to be companions with them. Regard not their societies, nor their scorns; their flatteries or their frowns; rejoice not with their joys, fear not their fear, care not their care, feed not on their dainties; get you up from among them, to your country, your city, where no unclean thing can enter or annoy. Live by faith, in the power of the Spirit, in the beauty of holiness, in the hope of the Gospel, in the joy of your God, in the magnificence, and yet the humility of the children of the great King.

II. Now, for a moment, let us consider THE EXCEEDING PRECIOUSNESS OF THIS GREAT MERCY, " I will be their God." I conceive that God, himself, could say no more than that. I do not think if the Infinite were to stretch his powers, and magnify his grace by some stupendous promise which could outdo every other, I do not believe that it could exceed in glory this promise, " I will be their God." Oh! Christian, do but consider what it is to have God to be thine own; consider what it is, compared with anything else.

> *Jacob's portion is the Lord;
> What can Jacob more require?
> What can heaven more afford—
> Or a creature more desire?"

Compare this portion with the lot of thy fellow-men! Some of them have their portion in the field, they are rich and increased in goods, and their yellow harvests are even now ripening in the sun; but what are harvests compared with thy God, the God of harvests? Or, what are granaries compared with him who is thy husbandman, and feeds thee with the bread of heaven? Some have their portion in the city; their wealth is superabundant, and in constant streams it flows to them, until they become a very reservoir of gold; but what is gold compared with thy God? Thou couldst not live on it; thy spiritual life could not be sustained by it. Apply it to thy aching head, and would it afford thee any ease? Put it on a troubled conscience, and could thy gold allay its pangs? Put it on thy desponding heart, and see if it could stay a solitary groan, or give thee one grief the less? But thou hast God, and in Him thou hast more than gold or riches e'er could buy, more than heaps of brilliant ore could ever purchase thee. Some have their portion in this world, in that which most men love, applause and fame; but ask thyself, is not thy God more to thee than that? What, if a thousand trumpets should blow thy praise, and if a myriad clarions should be loud with thine applause; what would it all be to thee if thou hadst lost thy God? Would this allay the turmoils of a soul ill at ease with itself? Would this prepare thee to pass the Jordan, and to breast those stormy waves which ere long must be forded by every man, when he is called from this world to lands unknown? Would a puff of wind serve thee then, or the clapping of the hands of thy fellow-creatures bless thee on thy dying bed? No, there are griefs here with which men cannot intermeddle, and there are griefs to come with which men cannot interfere to alleviate the pangs, and pains, and agonies, and dying strife. But when thou hast this—" I will be thy God "—thou hast as much as all other men can have put together; for this is all they have, and more. How little ought we to estimate the treasures of this world compared with God, when we consider that God frequently gives the worst riches to the worst of his creatures! As Luther said, God gives food to his children, and husks to his swine; and who are the swine that get the husks? It is not often that God's people get the riches of this world, and that does but prove that riches are little worth, else God would give them to us. Abraham gave the sons of Keturah a portion and sent them away; let me be Isaac and have my Father, and the world may take all the rest. Oh! Christian, ask for nothing in this world, but that thou mayest live on this, and that thou mayest die on this, "I will be their God. This exceedeth all the world besides.

But *compare this with what thou requirest, Christian.* What dost thou require? Is there not here all that thou dost require? To make thee happy thou wantest something that shall satisfy thee; and come I ask thee, is not this enough? Will not this fill thy pitcher to its very brim, aye, till it runs over? If thou canst put this promise inside thy cup, will not thou be forced to say, with David, "My cup runneth over; I have more than heart can wish?" When this is fulfilled, "I am thy God," let thy cup be ever so empty of earthly things, suppose thou hast not one solitary drop of creature joy, yet is not this enough to fill it until thy unsteady hand cannot hold the cup by reason of its fulness? I ask thee if thou art not complete when God is thine. Dost thou want anything but God? If thou thinkest thou dost, it were well for thee still to want; for all thou wantest save God, is but to gratify thy lust. Oh! Christian, is not this enough to satisfy thee if all else should fail?

But thou wantest more than quiet satisfaction; thou desirest, sometimes, rapturous delight. Come, soul, is there not enough here to delight thee? Put this promise to thy lips; didst e'er drink wine one-half so sweet as this, "I will be their God?" Didst ever harp or viol sound half so sweetly as this, "I will be their God?" Not all the music blown from sweet instruments, or drawn from living strings, could ever give such melody as this sweet promise, "I will be their God." Oh! here is a very sea of bliss, a very ocean of delight; come, bathe thy spirit in it; thou mayest swim, ay, to eternity, and never find a shore; thou may'st dive to the very infinite and never find the bottom, "*I will be their God.*" Oh! if this does not make thine eyes sparkle, if this make not thy foot dance for joy, and thy heart beat high with bliss, then assuredly thy soul is not in a healthy state.

But then thou wantest something more than present delights, something concerning which thou mayest exercise hope; and what more dost thou ever hope to get than the fulfilment of this great promise, "I will be their God?" Oh! hope, thou art a great-handed thing; thou layest hold of mighty things, which even faith hath not power to grasp; but though large thine hand may be, this fills it, so that thou canst carry nothing else. I protest, before God, I have not a hope beyond this promise. "O," say you, "you have a hope of heaven." Ay, I have a hope of heaven, but this is heaven—"I will be their God." What is heaven, but to be with God, to dwell with him, to realize that God is mine, and I am his? I say I have not a hope beyond that; there is not a promise beyond that; for all promises are couched in this, all hopes are included in this, "I will be their God." This is the master-piece of all promises; it is the top-stone of all the great and precious things, which God has provided for his children, "I will be their God." If we could really grasp it, if it could be applied to our soul and we could understand it, we might clap our hands and say, "Oh! the glory, oh! the glory, oh! the glory of that promise!" it makes a heaven below, and it must make a heaven above, for nothing else will be wanted but that, "I will be their God."

III. Now, for a moment, dwell on the CERTAINTY OF THIS PROMISE; it does not say, "I *may* be their God;" but "I *will* be their God." Nor does the text say, "Perhaps I shall be their God;" no, it says, "I *will* be their God." There is a sinner who says he won't have God for his God. He will have God to be his preserver, to take care of him, and keep him from accident. He does not object to having God to feed him, to give him his bread, and water, and raiment; nor does he mind making God somewhat of a showthing, that he may take out on Sunday, and bow before it, but he will not have God for his *God*; he will not take him to be his all. He makes his belly his God, gold his God, the world his God. How then is this promise to be fulfilled? There is one of God's chosen people there; he does not know that he is chosen yet, and he says he will not have God; how then is this

10

promise to be carried out? "Oh!" say some, "if the man wont have God, then, of course, God cannot get him;" and we have heard it preached, and we read it frequently, that salvation entirely depends upon man's will—that if man stands out and resists God's Holy Spirit, the creature can be the conqueror of the Creator, and finite power can overcome the infinite. Frequently I take up a book and I read, "Oh! sinner, be willing, for unless thou art, God cannot save thee;" and sometimes we are asked, "How is it that such an one is not saved?" And the answer is, "He is not willing to be; God strove with him, but he would not be saved." Ay, but suppose he had striven with him, as he did with those who *are* saved, would he have been saved then? "No, he would have resisted." Nay, we answer, it is not in man's will, it is not of the will of the flesh, nor of blood, but of the power of God; and we never can entertain such an absurd idea as, that man can conquer Omnipotence, that the might of man is greater than the might of God. We believe, indeed, that certain usual influences of the Holy Spirit may be overcome; we believe that there are general operations of the Spirit in many men's hearts which are resisted and rejected, but the effectual working of the Holy Ghost with the determination to save, could not be resisted, unless you suppose God overcome by his creatures, and the purpose of Deity frustrated by the will of man, which were to suppose something akin to blasphemy. Beloved, God has power to fulfil the promise, "I will be their God." "Oh!" cries the sinner, "I will not have thee for a God." "Wilt thou not?" says he, and he gives him over to the hand of Moses; Moses takes him a little and applies the club of the law, drags him to Sinai, where the mountain totters over his head, the lightnings flash, and thunders bellow, and then the sinner cries, "O God, save me!" "Ah! I thought thou wouldst not have me for a God?" "O Lord, thou shalt be my God," says the poor trembling sinner, "I have put away my ornaments from me; O Lord, what wilt thou do unto me? Save me! I will give myself to thee. Oh! take me!" "Ay," says the Lord, "I knew it; I said that I will be their God; and I have made thee willing in the day of my power." "I will be their God, and they shall be my people."

IV. Now, lastly, I said we would conclude, by URGING YOU TO MAKE USE OF GOD, if he be yours. It is strange that spiritual blessings are our only possessions that we do not employ. We get a great spiritual blessing, and we let the rust get on it for many a day. There is the mercy seat, for instance. Ah, my friends, if you had the cash box as full of riches as that mercy seat is, you would go often to it; as often as your necessities require. But you do not go to the mercy seat half so often as you need to go. Most precious things God has given to us, but we never over-use them. The truth is, they cannot be over-used; we cannot wear a promise thread-bare; we can never burn out the incense of grace; we can never use up the infinite treasures of God's loving kindness. But if *the blessings* God gives us are not used, perhaps *God* is the least used of all. Though he is our God, we apply ourselves less to him, than to any of his creatures, or any of his mercies, which he bestows upon us. Look at the poor heathen; they use their gods, though they be no gods. They put up a piece of wood or stone, and call it God; and how they use it! They want rain: the people assemble and ask for rain, in the firm but foolish hope that their god can give it. There is a battle, and their god is lifted up; he is brought out from the house, where he usually dwells, that he may go before them, and lead them on to victory. But how seldom do we ask counsel at the hands of the Lord! How often do we go about our business without asking his guidance! In our troubles how constantly do we strive to bear our burdens, instead of casting them upon the Lord, that he may sustain us! And this is not because we may not, for the Lord seems to say, "I am thine, soul, come and make use of me as thou wilt· thou mayest freely come to my store, and the oftener the better welcome." Have thou not a God lying by thee to no purpose; let not thy God be as other gods, serving only for a show: have not a name only that thou hast a God. Since he allows thee, having such a friend, use him daily. My God shall supply all your wants: never want whilst thou hast a God, never fear or faint whilst thou hast a God; go to thy treasure and take whatever thou needest; there is bread, and clothes, and health, and life, and all that thou needest. O Christian, learn the divine skill to make God all things, to make bread of thy God, and water, and health, and friends, and ease; he can supply thee with all these; or what is better, he can be instead of all these, thy food, thy clothing thy friend, thy life of thee. All this he hath said to thee in this one word, I am thy God; and hereupon thou mayest say, as a heaven-born saint once did, "I have no husband, and yet I am no widow, my Maker is my husband. I have no father or friend, and yet I am neither fatherless nor friendless; my God is both my father and my friend. I have no child, but is not he better to me than ten children? I have no house, but yet I have a home, I have made the Most High my habitation. I am left alone, but yet I am not alone, my God is good company for me; with him I can walk, with him I can take sweet counsel, find sweet repose; at my lying down, at my rising up, whilst I am in the house, or as I walk by the way, my God is ever with me; with him I travel, I dwell, I lodge, I live, and shall live for ever." Oh! child of God, let me urge thee to make use of thy God. Make use of him in prayer; I beseech thee, go to him often, because he is *thy* God. If he were another man's God, thou mightest weary him; but he is *thy* God. If he were my God and not thine, thou wouldst have no right to approach him, but he is *thy* God; he has made himself over to thee, if we may use such an expression, (and we think we may) he has become the positive property of all his children, so that all he has, and all he is, is theirs. O child, wilt thou let thy treasury lie idle, when thou wantest it? No; go and draw from it by prayer.

> "To him in every trouble flee,
> Thy best, thy only friend."

Fly to him, tell him all thy wants. Use him constantly by faith, at all times. Oh! I beseech thee, if some dark providence has come over thee, use thy God as a sun, for he is a sun. If some strong enemy has come out against thee, use thy God for a shield, for he is a shield to protect thee. If thou hast lost thy way in the mazes of life, use him as a guide, for the great Jehovah will direct thee. If thou art in storms, use him for the God who stilleth the raging of the sea, and saith unto the waves, "Be still." If thou art a poor thing, knowing not which way to turn, use him for a shepherd, for the Lord is thy Shepherd, and thou shalt not want. Whate'er thou art, where'er thou art, remember God is just what thou wantest, and he is just where thou wantest. I beseech thee, then, make use of thy God; do not forget him in thy trouble, but flee to him in the midst of thy distresses, and cry,

> "When all created streams are dried,
> Thy fulness is the same;
> May I with this be satisfied,
> And glory in thy name!
>
> No good in creatures can be found
> But may be found in thee;
> I must have all things, and abound,
> While God is God to me."

Lastly, Christian, let me urge thee again to use God to be thy delight this day. If thou hast trial, or if thou art free from it, I beseech thee make God thy delight; go from this house of prayer and be happy this day in the Lord. Remember it is a commandment, "Rejoice in the Lord, always, and again I say, rejoice." Do not be content to be moderately happy; seek to soar to the heights of bliss and to enjoy a heaven below; get near to God, and you will get near to heaven. It is not as it is with the sun here, the higher you go the colder you find it, because on the mountain there is nothing to reflect the rays of the sun; but with God, the nearer you go to him the brighter he will shine upon you, and when there are no other creatures to reflect his goodness, his light will be all the brighter. Go to God continually, importunately, confidently; "delight thyself also in the Lord and he shall bring it to pass;" "commit thy way unto the Lord, and he shall "guide thee by his counsel, and afterwards receive thee to glory."

Here is the first thing of the covenant; the second is like unto it. We will consider that another Sabbath-day. And now may God dismiss you with his blessing Amen.

Obedience Better than Sacrifice

"Behold, to obey is better than sacrifice, and to hearken than the fat of rams."
1 Samuel xv. 22.

Saul had been commanded to slay utterly all the Amalekites and their cattle. Instead of doing so, he preserved the king, and suffered his people to take the best of the oxen and of the sheep. When called to account for this, he declared that he did it with a view of offering sacrifice to God; but Samuel met him at once with the assurance that such sacrifices were no excuse for an act of direct rebellion, and in so doing he altered his sentence, which is worthy to be printed in letters of gold, and to be hung up before the eyes of the present generation: "To obey is better than sacrifice, and to hearken than the fat of rams."

I think that in this verse—and here I shall dwell mainly—there is first a voice to *professing Christians*, and then, secondly, to *unconverted persons*.

I. First, I will speak to you, my brothers and sisters in Christ Jesus, and who have made a PROFESSION of your faith in him.

Be it ever in your remembrance, that to obey, to keep strictly in the path of your Saviour's command, is better than any outward form of religion, and to hearken to his precept with an attentive ear is better than to bring the fat of rams, or anything else which you may wish to lay upon his altar.

Probably, there are some of you here to-night who may be living in the neglect of some known duty. It is no new thing for Christians to know their duty, to have their conscience enlightened about it, and yet to neglect it. If you are failing to keep the least of one of Christ's commands to his disciples, I pray you, brethren, be disobedient no longer. I know, for instance, that some of you can see it to be your duty, as believers, to be baptized. If you did not think it to be your duty, I would not bring this text to bear upon you; but if you feel it to be right, and you do it not, let me say to you that all the pretensions you make of attachment to your Master, and all the other actions which you may perform, are as nothing compared with the neglect of this. "To obey," even in the slightest and smallest thing, "is better than sacrifice," and to hearken diligently to the Lord's commands is better than the fat of rams. It may be that some of you, though you are professed Christians, are living in the prosecution of some evil trade, and your conscience has often said, "Get out of it." You are not in the position that a Christian ought to be in; but then you hope that you will be able to make a little money, and you will retire and do a world of good with it. Ah! God cares nothing for this rams' fat of yours; he asks not for these sacrifices which you intend to make. "To obey is better than sacrifice, and to hearken than the fat of rams." Perhaps you are in connection with a Christian church in which you may see much that is wrong, and you know that you ought not to tolerate it, but still you do so. You say, "I have a position of usefulness, and if I come out I shall not be so useful as I am now." My brother, your usefulness is but as the fat of rams, and "to obey is better than" it all. The right way for a Christian to walk in is to do what his Master bids him, leaving all consequences to the Almighty. You have nothing to do with your own usefulness further than to keep your Master's commands, at all hazards and under all risks. "I counsel thee to keep the King's commandments," and "whatsoever he saith unto thee, do it." Sit at his feet with Mary, and learn of him, and when thou risest up from that reverent posture, let it be with the prayer—

> "Help me to run in thy commands,
> 'Tis a delightful road;
> Nor let my head, nor heart, nor hands,
> Offend against my God."

Possibly, too, dear brother, there may be some evil habit in which you are indulging, and which you excuse by the reflection, "Well, I am always at the prayer meeting; I am constantly at communion, and I give so much of my substance to the support of the Lord's work." I am glad that you do these things; but oh! I pray you give up that sin! I pray you cut it to pieces and cast it away, for if you do not, all your show of sacrifice will be but an abomination. The first thing which God requires of you as his beloved is obedience; and though you should preach with the tongue of men and of angels, though you should give your body to be burned, and your goods to feed the poor, yet, if you do not hearken to your Lord, and are not obedient to his will, all besides shall profit you nothing. It is a blessed thing to be teachable as a little child, and to be willing to be taught of God; but it is a much more blessed thing still, when one has been taught to go at once and carry out the lesson which the Master has whispered in the ear. How many excellent Christians there are who sacrifice a goodly flock of sheep so as to replenish the altar of our God, who nevertheless are faulty because they obey not the word of the Lord. Look at our Missionary Society's list of subscribers, and ask yourself the question, Do all these help the spread of the gospel by obedience to the precept, "Go ye into all the world and preach the gospel to every creature"? There you see in the money gift the sacrifice, but better far to have obedience. Both ought to be joined together; but of the two, better is the act of obedience than of giving. Noah's sacrifice sent up a sweet savour before God, but in God's sight the obedience which led him to build the ark and enter in with his family was far more precious; and for this his name is written amongst the champions of faith, and handed down to us as a word of honour and renown.

Moreover, brethren, to obey is better than sacrifice in the matter of caring for the sick and needy of all classes. We rejoice in the number of hospitals which adorn our cities. These are the princely trophies of the power of our holy religion. To these we triumphantly point as amongst the ripe fruits of that Christianity which is for the healing of the nations, chiefly in a spiritual, but also in the physical aspect of man's diseased and woe-begone state. There are no nobler words in our language than those inscribed on so many walls—" Supported by voluntary contributions." We glory in them. Rome's monuments, Grecian trophies, Egyptia's mighty tombs, and Assyria's huge mono-liths, are dwarfed into petty exhibitions of human pride and vanity before the sublime majesty of these exhibitions of a God-given love to our fellow men ; but all these homes of mercy and healing become evils to ourselves though they are blessings to the distressed, if we con-tribute of our wealth to their exchequer and neglect personally to visit the fatherless and widows in their affliction, to feed the hungry, to care for the sick, and do not, like the Master, go about doing good. Give as God has given to you; but remember God acts as well as gives. " Go thou and do likewise." Sacrifice, but also obey. A cup of cold water given to a disciple in the name of a disciple, and in obedience to the Lord, is a golden deed, valued by our heavenly Master above all price, more precious in his sight than silver, yea, than much fine gold. May I put this very earnestly to the members of this church, and, indeed, to all of you who hope that you are followers of Christ? Is there anything that you are neglecting? Is there any sin in which you are indulging? Is there any voice of conscience to which you have turned a deaf ear? Is there one passage of Scripture which you dare not look in the face, because you are living in neglect of it? Then let Samuel's voice come to you, and set you seeking for more grace; for "to obey is better than sacrifice, and to hearken than the fat of rams."

II. But my main business to-night is with the UNCONVERTED; and may the Master give us grace to deal with them affectionately, faith-fully, and earnestly!

My hearer, in the first place, God has given to you in the gospel dispensation a command. It is a command in the obeying of which there is eternal life, and the neglect of which will be and must be your everlasting ruin. That command is this : " Believe on the Lord Jesus Christ, and thou shalt be saved." The gospel does not come to you as the law does, and say, " This do, and thou shalt live;" but it speaks as in the language of Isaiah the prophet, and says, " Hearken diligently unto me; hear, and your souls shall live." It tells you that whosoever be-lieveth that Jesus is the Christ is born of God, and it bids the heralds of the cross go out and cry, " He that believeth and is baptized shall be saved; he that believeth not shall be damned." To use the expressive language of the beloved apostle John, " This is his commandment, That we should believe on the name of his Son Jesus Christ." To believe is to trust, to trust with your whole heart; and whosoever trusts in the Lord Jesus Christ with his whole heart has the promise of eternal life; nay, if that act be sincere, it is the result of eternal life already given. God, the just One, must punish sin, therefore he must punish you; but Jesus Christ became man, and stood and smarted in the sinner's place, that whosoever trusteth in him might neither smart nor suffer, because God punished Christ in the stead of every man who comes to Christ and rests upon him. To trust in Jesus, therefore, is God's first and great commandment of salvation. Now, hark thee, sinner! God commands thee to keep this, and surely he has a right to do so. If he wills to save, he has a sovereign right to choose his own way of saving. If a man gives to the poor he may do so as he wills, whether he gives at this door or at that, or through the window; and so God is pleased to use the door of simple faith as the only door through which to bestow mercy on the sons of men.

And not only has he a right to choose this way, but it is the only way that would suit you. If God determined to save none but those who kept his law, what would become of you? If he only gave grace to the holy and to the good, where would you be? But the way of faith suits, and readily suits one who has broken God's commands. Though a sinner be dying, though he may be on the cross like the dying thief, yet, as the way of salvation is but a looking at Christ, there is hope for him even in the last extremity that he may still be able to look and live. Why should you kick against God's way when it is the best to suit you, when none can be more suitable, none more simple? He has chosen it because it is a way which honours his dear Son. Your trusting Jesus gives glory to Jesus, and therefore God delights in your faith. And, besides, it brings a blessing to your own soul. To trust in Christ is in itself a boon. It is humbling, but it is comforting. It empties you, but it fills you; it strips you, but it clothes you. Faith has a double action like a two-edged sword. It kills pride, but at the same time it heals the wound it gave by giving to the sinner trust in Jesus. To confide Jesus is the best conceivable way I can imagine by which a sinner can be reconciled unto God through the blood of the great Redeemer. I pray thee, therefore, be not thou angry because God is gracious, and be not thou rebellious when the still small voice saith, "Look, sinner, look to him who died upon the tree, and by that look thou shalt live."

Now, this first point being clear, that God has given a command, the second remark is that the most of men, instead of obeying God, *want to bring him sacrifice*. They suppose that their own way of salvation is much better than any that the Almighty can have devised, and therefore they offer their fat of rams. This takes different forms, but it is always the same principle. One man says, "Well now, I will give up my pleasures; you shall not see me at the ball-room, you shall not catch me at the theatre, I will forsake the music-hall, you shall not discover me in low company; I will give up all the things that my heart calls good, and will not that save me?" No, it will not. When you have made all this sacrifice, all I shall or can say of it is, "To obey is better than sacrifice." "Well, but suppose I begin to attend a place of worship? Suppose I go very regularly, and as often as the doors are opened? Suppose I go to early matins, and to the even-song? Suppose I attend every day in the week where the bell is always going? Suppose I come to the sacrament, and am baptized? Supposing I go through with the thing, and give myself thoroughly up to all outward observances; will not all this save me?" No, nor will it even help you to being saved. These things will no more save you than husks will fill your hungry belly. It is not the husks you want, you want the kernels; and so, poor soul, you do not want external ceremonies, you want the inward substance, and you will never get that except by trusting Jesus Christ. There was a time when doctrine was far more highly valued than is now the case with some Christians. You will often meet with those who seem to value men by their contributions to church funds rather than by their soundness in the faith. Now, if I am to judge men at all, I prize the man who hearkens to God's voice far more than the one who can bring the "fat of rams" to the altar of God's house. A rich heretic I would reject and put from me, while the poor but obedient God-fearing disciple I would welcome with all my heart. An ear ever open to listen to God's voice, a heart ever soft to receive the impress of God's teaching,—these are far more precious than a hand full of silver and gold, and a mouth promising large things. For "to hearken is better than the fat of rams." All the costly gifts cast into the treasury are valuable chiefly as representing an inner spirit of devotion, and of self-consecration. They may exist as outward acts without the living spirit which gives them value in God's eyes. We need therefore to cultivate the soul, and to see that that sacred spirit of devout submission dwells within us which dwelt in him, who not only sacrificed himself on the cross, being obedient unto death, but ever lived in that state of heart which was embodied in his prayer, "Nevertheless, not my will but thine be done." Would the washing of the windows of a house make the inhabitants thereof clean? Yea, does the painting and ornamenting of the exterior of a mansion make the dwellers in it healthier or holier men? We read of devils entering into a clean swept and garnished house, and the last end of that man was worse than the first. All the outward cleansing is but the gilding of the bars of the cage full of unclean birds; the whitewashing of sepulchres full of rottenness and dead men's bones. Washing the outside of a box will leave all the clothes inside as foul as ever. Remember therefore that all that you can do in the way of outward religion is nothing but the sacrifice of the fat of rams; and "to obey is better than sacrifice, and to hearken than the fat of rams."

"Yes," says another, "but suppose I punish myself a good deal for all that I have done? I will abstain from this, I will deny myself that, I will mortify myself in this passion, I will give up that evil." Friend, if thou hast any evil give it up; but when thou hast done so do not rely upon that, for this oughtest thou to have done, and not to have left the other undone. God's command is "Believe," and if thou shouldest go about to sacrifice thy lusts till they lie bleeding like a hecatomb of bullocks upon the altar, yet I must say to thee, as Samuel sternly said to Saul, "To obey is better than to sacrifice, and to hearken to the gospel message is better than all this fat of rams."

But it is thought by some if they should add to all this a good deal of generosity, surely they will be saved. "Suppose I give money to the poor, build a lot of alms-houses, and help to build a church, suppose I am generous even beyond my means, will not this help me?" Sinner, why wilt thou ask such a question? God has set before thee a door an open door, and over it is written, "Believe and live," and yet thou goest about and gaddest abroad to find another door! What is all thy gold worth, man? Why, heaven is paved with it! All the gold thou hast would not buy a single slab of the eternal pavement, and dost thou think to enter there by dint of thy poor giving? If he were hungry he would not tell thee, for his are the cattle on a thousand hills, and his are the mines of silver, and the sparkling ores of gold. The diamond, and the topaz, and the chrysolite, are all his own, and his eye sees them hidden in their secret veins and lodes, and dost thou think to bribe the Eternal with thy paltry purse? Oh! Do thou understand that "To obey is better than sacrifice, and to hearken than the fat of rams."

"Yes, but," saith the sinner, "if I could add to all this a great deal of confidence in those good men who are recognised by the world as priests? Suppose I put myself into their bonds? I would not go to the Roman Catholics, for I do not like them much, but supposing I go to the Episcopalians—for they have priests too, and sprinkle children with holy water, and bury the reprobate dead,' in 'sure and certain hope of a glorious resurrection to everlasting life'—could not they do something for me? Or suppose I go to some Dissenting minister, and put myself under his care, cannot he help me?" No, sir, there is nought in us that can help you one jot. We hate the very thought of being priests; I would sooner be a devil than be a priest, with the exception of being what all Christians are—priests unto God. Let me justify that strong remark; of all pretensions on earth, there is none so detestable as the pretence of being able to bestow grace upon men, and of standing between their souls and God. Beloved, we are your servants for Christ's sake, but as for any priestly authority to give grace to you, we shake off the imputation as Paul shook off the viper from his hand into the fire. We speak to men of our own kith and kin, we talk to you out of warm earnest hearts, but we can only say to you, "Do not trust in us, for you will be fools if you do. Do not trust in any man, for though you might make a sacrifice of your reason by so doing, yet remember that "to obey is better than sacrifice." God demands of you, not submission to your fellow-men, whoever they may be; he requires of you not to listen to the pealing of organs, not to attend gorgeous ceremonies where the smoke of incense goes up in gaudy palaces dedicated to his service; but he requires this, that you believe in the Lord Jesus Christ, and then he tells you that you shall live. Trust the Saviour and you shall not perish, neither shall any pluck you out of his hand. But if you refuse this way of salvation, then there is none other presented to you, and you must perish in your sins.

"To obey is better than sacrifice, and to hearken than the fat of rams." And now I have to show that *it is so*. Men are always setting up these ways of salvation of their own, and they will run anywhere sooner than come to Christ and do as God tells them. Let me show how to obey is better than sacrifice, and how to hearken is better than the fat of rams.

It is better in itself. It shows that you are more *humble*. There are persons in the world who say that to trust Christ to save us from sin is not to be humble. Now, is it not always humility on the part of a child to do exactly what its parent tells it without asking any questions? I think it is so. Some poor Papists go down on their knees, and even lick the dust to do penance, and they think that this is being humble. Now, suppose one of your children has offended you, and you say to him, " Come, my dear, I freely forgive you; come and give me a kiss, and it is all over." He shakes his head, and says, " No, father, I cannot kiss you;" and he runs away upstairs and shuts himself up. You knock at the door, and say, " Come, my child, come and kiss me, and it is all forgiven." But he shakes his head and says, " No, never." He shuts himself up there all alone, and he thinks he is doing more to put away your anger by so doing than by obeying your command. You say to him solemnly, " My child, I will chasten you again for disobedience if you do not come and accept the forgiveness which I offer to you if you will but kiss me." The child sullenly says, " No, father, I will do something else that is more humbling;" and then you feel in your soul that that is an unhumbled child or else he would at once do what his father told him, without thinking whether it would be a humiliating thing or not. It would be a humbling thing because his father told him to do it, and if he were a right-minded child he would do it from a spirit of obedience. Now, you may think it very humble on your part to want to feel a great deal of conviction, and to shed a great many tears, and to pray a great many prayers, but the most lowly thing you can do is to perform what the Master tells you. " Trust me," saith he; " do not go over there to weep; come unto me, all ye that labour and are heavy laden, and I will give you rest." Do not stand at the swine's trough saying, "I will not arise and go to my Father, for I am not fit to go till I have suffered a great deal more;" but hear the voice which bids thee say, " I will arise and go unto my Father, and what I have to say I will say unto him, and if I have to weep I will weep with my head in his bosom, while I receive the kisses of his love." Come, poor sinner, do not set up thy proud humility in the teeth of God; but, since he bids thee look and live, oh! give up thy prayers, and even thy tears, and thy repentings, and thy convictions—have done with them all as grounds of confidence, and look to Jesus Christ, and to Jesus Christ alone.

But in the next place, *it is really a more holy thing.* There are some soldiers here to-night. Now, suppose one of these received orders from the commanding officer to keep guard at such and such a door. All of a sudden he thinks to himself, " I am very fond of our commander, and I should like to do something for him." He puts his musket against the wall, and starts out to find a shop where he can buy a bunch of flowers. He is away from his post all the while, of course, and when he comes back he is discovered to have been away from the post of duty. He says, " Here is the bunch of flowers I went to get;" but I hear his officer say, " To obey is better than that; we cannot allow you—military discipline would not permit it—to run off at every whim and wish of yours and neglect your duty, for who knows what mischief might ensue?" The man, however much you might admire what he was doing, would certainly be made to learn by military law that "To obey is better than sacrifice." It is a holier and a better thing to do one's duty than to make duties for one's self and then set about them. Now, does it not seem a very pretty thing when a man puts on a very handsome-looking gown with a yellow cross down his back, and something else in pink, and I know not what colours, and ministers in a place decorated with flowers, and where there are such sweet things, incense smoking from silver censers and choristers all in white, is not that man serving God? When he preaches he does not say to the people, "Believe and live;" but begins to talk about "The blessed sacrament of the altar," or some other such stuff? Is he not serving God when he does this? I will appeal to this old Book. Where inside these leaves and covers is there a word about burning this smoking incense? When did Christ ever say anything about it? Where have we anything about that decorated font, or about that pulpit that looks so very glorious? Why, the man has been making up a spiritual pantomime for himself, and he has left out altogether the soul of the matter. He has left out Christ, and therefore he has not done his work. He has done twenty other things, I dare say very sincerely, and with a very pure desire, but after all he wants to be made to learn the meaning of this passage, "To obey is better than sacrifice, and to hearken than the fat of rams;" and better than smoking incense, and flowers, and gilded crosses, and chasubles, and albs, and dalmatics, and all such things as could possibly be brought together. If he had God's Word for it it would be right, but without God's Word it is a mere invention of man to which God can have no regard. It is a more holy thing to do what God bids you, than to do what you yourselves invent. When I have done what I have invented, however pretty it may be, however venerable it may seem, yet what does it come to? Suppose I worship God in one of those smart robes, is my worship a bit the better? Suppose I should go home to-night and spend the night on my knees, and think that by that means I should satisfy God? What should I have done but made my knees ache? Supposing I had filled this place with incense, what should I have done but probably have made you cough? Suppose I had decorated myself and this place, some of you might have been pleased, but what connection on earth can there be between flowers and holiness, or between gilding and millinery and glorifying God? If our God were like to some of the fabled deities of Greece and Rome, he might be delighted with these pretty things, but our God is in the heavens, and when he does show his splendour he scatters stars broadcast across the sky with both his hands, and what are all your prettinesses to him? What is your swelling music and all your pretty things to him who built the heavens and piled the earth with all its rugged splendour of forest, and mountain, and stream? "To obey is better than sacrifice, and to hearken than the fat of rams?"

But while I remark upon these things, let me also say that to obey the precept "Believe and live" is certainly a great deal more effectual to the soul's salvation than all the sacrifice and all the fat of rams which you can offer. Let me give you a picture by way of illustration. Naaman was a leper. He desired healing. The prophet said to him, "Go and wash in Jordan seven times, and thou shalt be clean." Now Naaman thought within himself, "I dare say; wash! does he think me to be some filthy wretch who wants washing? He says I must wash seven times! Does he really think that I have not washed for so long that it will take seven washings to get me clean? He says I must wash! What a simple thing! I have washed every day, and it has done me no good. He says I must wash in Jordan! Are not Abana and Pharpar, rivers of Damascus, better than all the waters of Jordan? Why cannot I wash in them and be clean?" This is just what some of you say about believing. You say, "Well, but sacraments there must be something in them! Believing in Christ—why it is such a simple thing! I am such a respectable person. This is a very good religion to preach to thieves and so on, but surely you forget that I have a great many good works of my own; cannot I think of them? You say I must trust in Christ, as though you thought nothing of my good works." Well, you are near the mark, sir. I do not think anything of them; I would not give a penny for a waggon-load of them. The whole of them are just what Paul calls them—"refuse." He says, "I count them but dung that I may win Christ, and be found in him." All your best works are but so much rubbish to be carted out of the way, and if you trust in them they will be your ruin, and all we say to you is, "BELIEVE AND LIVE." Now Naaman was in a great rage, and he went away, but his servant said to him, "My father, if the prophet had bidden thee do some great thing wouldest thou not have done it? Much rather, then, wilt thou not do what he tells thee when he says, Wash and be clean?" Now, if my Master were to say to you to-night, "Walk to the city of York barefoot and you shall be saved;" if you believed it, the most of you would start off to-night; but when the message is, "Believe and live," oh! that is too simple! What! just trust Christ and be saved on the spot? Why, it cannot be, you think. If we bade you do some great thing you would do it, but you refuse to do so simple a thing as to believe. But if Naaman had gone to Abana and Pharpar he would not have been healed, and if he had sought out all the physicians in Syria and paid away all his money, he would have been white with leprosy still. There was nothing but washing in Jordan that would heal him. And so with you, sinner, you may go and do fifty thousand things, but you will never get your sins forgiven, and you never, *never* shall have a hope of heaven unless you will obey this one precept: "Believe on the Lord Jesus Christ," but if you do this you shall find that "to obey is better than sacrifice" indeed, and "to hearken than" all "the fat of rams."

But now we must close with a remark which we have made over and over again during this discourse, namely, that *not obeying and not hearkening to the gospel, sinner, you must perish.* I know that some think it rather hard that there should be nothing for them but ruin if they will not believe in Jesus Christ, but if you will think for a minute you will see that it is just and reasonable. I suppose there is no way for a man to keep his strength up except by eating. If you were to say, "I shall never eat, I will not take refreshment," you might go to Madeira, or travel to all the climates, (supposing you lived long enough!) but you would most certainly find that no climate and no exercise would avail to keep you alive if you refused to eat; and would you then say, "Well, it is a hard thing that I should die because I refused to eat"? It is not an unjust thing that if you are such a fool as not to eat, you must die. It is precisely so with believing. "Believe, and thou art saved." If thou wilt not believe, it is no hard thing that thou shouldst be damned! It would be harder if it were not to be the case. There is a man who is thirsty, and there stands before him a fountain. "No," he says, "I will never touch a drop of moisture as long as I live; cannot I get my thirst quenched in some other way?" We tell him, no; he must drink or die. He says, "I will never drink, but it is a hard thing that I must therefore die, a very hard thing." No, it is not, poor simpleton; it is nothing but an inevitable law of nature. Thou must drink or die; why play the fool at such a cost as that? Drink, man, drink! And so with Christ. There is the way of salvation, and thou must trust Christ or perish; and there is nothing hard in it that thou shouldst perish if thou dost not. Here is a man out at sea; he has got a chart, and that chart, if well studied, will, with the help of the compass, guide him to his journey's end. The pole-star gleams out amidst the cloud-rifts, and that, too, will help him. "No," says he, "I will have nothing to do with your stars; I do not believe in the North Pole; I shall not attend to that little thing inside the box; one needle is as good as another needle; I do not believe in your rubbish, and I will have nothing to do with it; it is only a lot of nonsense got up by people on purpose to make money, and I will have nothing to do with it." The man does not get to shore anywhere; he drifts about, but never reaches port, and he says it is a very hard thing, a very hard thing. I do not think so. So some of you say, "Well, I am not going to read your Bible; I am not going to listen to your talk about Jesus Christ; I do not believe in such things." You will be damned, then, sir! "That's very hard," say you. No, it is not.

It is not more so than the fact that if you reject the compass and the pole-star you will not get to your journey's end. There is no help for it; it must be so; you say you will have nothing to do with these things, and you pooh-pooh them. You will find it a very hard thing to laugh these matters down when you come to die, when the cold, clammy sweat must be wiped from your brow, and your heart beats against your ribs as if it wanted to get out and get away to God. Oh soul! you will find then, that these Sundays, and these services, and this preaching, and this old Book, are something more and better than you thought they were, and you will wonder that you were so simple as to neglect them, the only guides to salvation; and above all, that you neglected Christ, that Pole-star which alone shines aloft to guide the mariner to the port of peace. Now, where do you live to-night? You live, perhaps, the other side of London Bridge, and you have to get over there to-night as you go home; but while you have been sitting here you have got a fancy into your head that you do not believe in bridges, and you do not believe in boats, and you do not believe in water. You say, "I am not going over any of your bridges; do not tell me; I shall not get into any of your boats; if there is a river, I am not going over it; I do not believe in crossing rivers." You go along, and you come to the bridge, but you will not cross it; there is a boat, but you will not get into it; there is the river, and you say you will not cross that anyhow, and yet you think it is very hard that you cannot get home. Now, I think you must have got something that has over-balanced your reasoning powers, for you would not think it so hard if you were in your senses. If a man will not do the thing that is necessary to a certain end I do not see how he can expect to gain that end. You have taken poison, and the physician brings an antidote, and says, "Take it quickly, or you will die; but if you take it quickly, I will guarantee that the poison will be neutralised." But you say, "No, doctor, I do not believe it; let everything take its course; let every tub stand on its own bottom; I will have nothing to do with you, doctor." "Well, sir, you will die, and when the coroner's inquest is held on your body, the verdict will be, 'Served him right!' So will it be with you if, having heard the gospel of Jesus Christ, you say, "Oh! pooh-pooh! I am too much of a common-sense man to have anything to do with that, and I shall not attend to it." Then, when you perish, the verdict given by your conscience, which will sit upon the King's quest at last, will be a verdict of "*Felo-de-se*"—"he destroyed himself." So says the old Book—"O Israel, thou hast destroyed thyself!"

But when I quote that text I must not stop there, for the next line is, "but in me is thy help found." Oh! my dear hearer, what a mercy it is that there is help in God! There is help in God for you. There is help in God for the worst of you. I cannot tell who there may be here to-night. There may be some who have sinned very greatly, but there is help laid upon one who is "mighty to save." Where are you, big sinner? Here is a great Saviour able to put all your sins away. Have you grown grey in wickedness? Ah! my Master can put away seventy years of sin by a moment's application of his precious blood. See him bleeding on the cross in agonies so great, that angels might have wept to gaze upon him.

> "See from his head, his hands, his feet,
> Sorrow and love flow mingled down!
> Did e'er such love and sorrow meet,
> Or thorns compose so rich a crown?"

There must be merit in such mighty agonies. If thou trustest in the merits of that precious blood thou shalt one day be with him in Paradise. God give thee to trust Jesus, to trust Jesus now, and then we shall meet again where they sing, " Unto him that loved us, and washed us from our sins in his own blood, be glory for ever and ever. Amen."

> "Behold the Lamb of God!
> Behold, believe and live;
> Behold his all-atoning blood,
> And life receive.
>
> Look from thyself to him,
> Behold him on the tree;
> What though the eye of faith be dim?
> He looks on thee.
>
> That meek, that languid eye,
> Turns from himself away;
> Invites the trembling sinner nigh,
> And bids him stay.
>
> Stay with him near the tree,
> Stay with him near the tomb;
> Stay till the risen Lord you see,
> Stay 'till he come.'"

PORTION OF SCRIPTURE READ BEFORE SERMON—1 Samuel xv.

A Clear Conscience

"Then shall I not be ashamed, when I have respect unto all thy commandments."
—Psalm cxix. 6.

ANY attempt to keep the law of God with the view of being saved thereby is sure to end in failure. So contrary is it to the express warnings of the divine Lawgiver, and so much does it run counter to the whole gospel, that he who ventures to seek justification by his own merits ought to be ashamed of his presumption. When God tells us that salvation is not by the works of the law, art thou not ashamed of trying to procure it by thy obedience to its precepts? When he declares that by the works of the law there shall no flesh be justified in his sight, art thou not ashamed to go and seek after justification where he tells thee it never can be found? When he over and over again declares that salvation is by faith, and that it is a matter of grace to be received, dost thou not blush for thyself that thou shouldst give the lie to God, and propound a righteousness of thine own conceit, in which thou hast vainly tried to keep up a respectable appearance, screening the palpable delinquencies of thy life under a thin veil of piety toward God and charity toward men? Eternal life is not to be earned by any trade you can carry on in works of the flesh; because, however estimable in the opinion of men, they are simply execrable in the sight of God. If a man seeks to keep the commandments of God in order that he may attain eternal life thereby, he will be ashamed and confounded. He had better at once renounce the folly of attempting so insane, so futile, so impossible a task as that of defending his own cause and justifying his own soul. But when a man is converted, when he has believed in Christ Jesus to the salvation of his soul, when he is justified by faith and his sin is blotted out, when he has obtained mercy, found grace in the eyes of the Lord, and entered into the rest of faith, because he knows that he is a saved man, then in keeping the precepts of the law he will gratify a strong inclination. In fact, it henceforth becomes his highest ambition to be obedient, and the great delight of his soul is to run in the ways of God's commandments out of gratitude for the great benefits he has received. And let it never be imagined that, because Christ has redeemed us from the curse of the law, there is therefore a complete removal of all moral constraints and restraints from Christian men. We are not under the law, but under grace, yet are we not lawless and libertine, since we have become servants of God and followers of Christ. Nay, but we are under another law—a law of another sort, which works upon us after another fashion. What if a man says, "I am free from the police, and the magistrate, and the judge, and the executioner," does it therefore follow that he is free from the rules of his father's house? Assuredly not. The child may be quite clear of the police court, but there is a rod at home. There is a father's smile; there is a father's frown. And though Christians shall never be so punished for their sins that they can come under condemnation, seeing they are clean delivered from that evil calamity by Christ, yet being children of God they come under another discipline—the discipline of his house and home—a discipline of chastisements not at all of a legal caste; for, however bitter the suffering it often entails, though he cause grief he will have compassion; the rebukes are sharp, but the retribution is not vindictive: and the Lord is wont to smile with approbation, to speak with commendation, and to bestow his compensations with liberal hand on those who seek his face, hearken to his voice, and do his bidding. When he has committed to us some service which he only could qualify us to discharge, he has often caused us to partake of the fruits in abundant joy. Now, I shall endeavour to bring out this principle while I am speaking upon our text. Those who are children of God should seek after universal obedience to the divine commands. They should have respect unto all the Lord's commandments. If they do so they will have a full requital; and this is the reward. "Then shall I not be ashamed, when I have respect unto all thy commandments."

Two things, then, claim our attention: *the universality of believing obedience*, and *the excellence of its result*.

I. THE UNIVERSALITY OF BELIEVING OBEDIENCE is here highly commended.

The esteem in which we hold, and the tribute we pay to, all God's commandments is spoken of. Not some of his commandments, but all of them—not picking and choosing—paying attention to this, because it pleases me, and omitting that, because it is not equally pleasurable, but the careful, earnest respecting of all the statutes of God and the anxious endeavour to keep them all—this it is which challenges attention.

Therein is *great blessedness*. Turn to the psalm itself, which is far preferable to any reflections we could offer, inasmuch as the word of God must ever excel the word of man. There David says, "Blessed are the undefiled in the way, who walk in the law of the Lord." Cometh this blessedness simply on those who are in the way, irrespective of their walk and conversation? Nay, but let them take heed lest they step aside and put their foot into the puddle and stain their garments. The persons who are truly blessed are the undefiled who so watch their walk that they endeavour in everything to adorn the doctrine of God their Saviour, and in nothing to grieve the Spirit of God. There lies the blessedness, not in partial obedience, but in perfect obedience as far as it can be attained; not now and then, but ever and anon; not in some things, but in all things, as far as we are taught of the living God. The only way to avoid defilement is to have respect and pay deference to all the commandments of the Lord. Whether we observe it or not, there is never an omission of duty or a commission of fault that does not cast a stain upon the purity of conscience and the integrity of character. Wouldest thou wish to be spotted from head to foot, believer? I know thou wouldest not. If thou wouldest be blest, thou must be undefiled, and if thou wouldest be undefiled, there must be a universality about thy obedience—walking in all the commandments of the Lord.

To enjoy this beatitude a holy walking must become habitual. This sacred exercise is very different from sluggish piety. "Blessed are the undefiled in the way who walk in the law of the Lord." A man may sit down in the road without soiling his skin or fouling his apparel, but that is not enough. There must be progress—practical action— in the Christian life; and in order to blessedness we must be doing something for the Master. Slothfulness is not the way to blessedness. Nor can we serve the Lord in this active work except we labour in all things to mind his will, and walk according to his way. God is to be sought diligently by sincere souls. "Blessed are they that keep his testimonies and that seek him with the whole heart." Now, you cannot keep the testimonies, and know the doctrine, unless you have the will in full force and vigorous energy. It seems to be almost as inevitable as a law of nature that a man who is not sound in his life cannot be sound in his judgment. Wisdom will not long hold a seat in the head of that man who has yielded up his heart to folly. A pure theology and a loose morality will never blend. We have known men who thought themselves mightily orthodox indulge in many unseemly and profligate habits; in fact, they have made light of their own sins: but that boasted orthodoxy of theirs presently develops into some pernicious fallacy. Be assured of it, you cannot keep the testimonies unless you be willing to keep the precepts. Vaunt as ye may your knowledge of the *letter* of the Scriptures, you shall fail to be owned of God as his witnesses, unless there is the witness of the life as well as the witness of the lips. And how can the witness of the life be sincere unless we strive in all things to keep the statutes of the Lord? How can we be said to serve him with our whole heart if part of our heart goes after vanity— if we hug some favourite sin, or if we leave some known duty in abeyance, saying, "When we have a more convenient season we will attend to thee." No, the blessedness is to the undefiled. The blessedness is to the walkers in the way. The blessedness is to the keepers of the divine testimonies. The blessedness is to those that seek the Lord with their whole heart. So, you see, you must take care to have respect unto all the commandments if you are to get the blessedness of the Christian life.

If you will carefully notice the fourth verse of this psalm you will see that this keeping of *all the commandments* is itself a positive command of God: "Thou hast commanded us to keep thy precepts diligently." That is enough warrant for a Christian—"Thou hast commanded." Now, the command of God to his people is not, "Ye shall keep some of my commands, and walk in a measure according to my mind, and after my will." What father is there who will say to his chidlren, "You must sometimes obey me. The rule of my house is that you may use your own discretion, and follow your own inclination as to which of my injunctions you obey and which you neglect; you can have your own way at times, if you will but occasionally yield to me in a few things." Such a father would be quite unworthy to be at the head of any household. Certainly our heavenly Father is not thus lax in his discipline. He has spoken to his children in tones of love. The law of his mouth has been given as a light to illuminate our path, and as a lamp to guide our feet. So palpable, then, is the divine benevolence that the more imperious his voice, the more interested we must be in heeding it. Does he say then—"Thou shalt keep my statutes and observe my ordinances."—doubt not for an instant that there is much profit in following the instructions closely, and great peril in disregarding them. And inasmuch as the authority of God goes with each command, with one precept as well as another, therefore should it be the object of the Christian that he should keep all the commands. He should make no choice, or selection, as to the words of the Lord, but take them all, and pray the Lord to bring him into conformity with every one of them.

That this is a meet and proper subject of prayer becomes very obvious; for in the next verse the psalmist exclaims, "Oh that my ways were directed to keep thy statutes!"

Now, no man I think ever prayed God to grant him partial obedience. Did he ever pray, dare he ever pray, "O Lord, help me to overcome some of my sins, but not all. This day preserve me from some temptations, but allow me to indulge some of my propensities"? Did you ever pray, "O Lord, keep me, I pray thee, from great and open sins, but permit me in thine infinite mercy to enjoy certain private sins, that I am exceedingly fond of"? Such a prayer were worthier of a worshipper of the devil than of a worshipper of God. No; our heart renewed by grace craves to be perfectly set free from sin. We have not obtained it; we are pressing on towards it, but this, even now, is our desire, and our prayer. Hence you cannot wonder that in the text the believing man is spoken of as having respect unto all God's commandments, since, if it be a matter of prayer, it cannot be in respect to some of God's commandments, but he must pray that he may have respect to everyone of them.

Now, I want to come a little closer to details. What do we mean by having respect to all God's commandments? I reply that, whatever there is that the Lord has spoken in any part of his word we desire to hold in devout esteem, and to have respect to every utterance of his will. The law, as he gave it to Moses, is no longer to us the way of obtaining life, but it is still in the hands of Christ a most blessed rule of living. It is divided into two tablets, and our prayer is that we should keep them both, reverently observing them; that towards God our life should ever be obedient, truthful, adoring: that we should have respect unto him in all our ways; that we should lean upon him; that we should depend upon him; that then we should serve him, and devote ourselves wholly to him. To seek his glory, first and foremost, is the chief end of our being. We must not forget this. But then there follow six commands upon the other stone, which relate to men, and we must mind them; for it were a poor thing to say, " I am devout towards God, but I care not to be just towards men." A devout thief would be a strange anomaly; an adoring murderer were a singular incongruity; a disciple of the Lord Jesus Christ indulging in covetousness is a self-evident contradiction. No, he that loves God must love his neighbour as himself; and I do trust our desire is that we may not fail in obedience to either of these tables, but may by the work of the Holy Spirit in us be wrought into an uprightness of conversation and character, both towards God and towards men. Some commands of God are highly spiritual, while others may be described rather as moral. Surely, to trust God is one of the grand commands. " Believe in the Lord Jesus Christ, and thou shalt be saved " is a precept which we would never wittingly neglect. " Trust in the Lord with all thine heart, and lean not to thine own understanding." " Cast your care on him." " Draw near unto him." All such spiritual exhortations as these relate to the life of the quickened believer. God has forbidden us to disregard, to despise, or to disparage any one of them. Oh that we may abound in all the graces of the Spirit, and be diligent in all the acts of our spiritual life. But we must not, therefore, forget or be negligent concerning morals, which some have accounted to be minor obligations, pretending to abound in prayer, but positively slothful in business, content to wait but not to work. They said that they were serving at the altar, but we saw that they were indolent enough in the shop. Christian men who stand up for the truth should take care not to be lax in their conduct when they are so wonderfully strict in their creed. Do not trifle with truth in speaking to your fellow man while you insist on respecting the truth of God. Can anything be more despicable than the pietists who prate much about the faithfulness of God's promises, but are not very particular about keeping their own promises? They say that they will let you have an article home on Friday night, and you do not get it till the following Wednesday; that is telling a falsehood. If you saw yourselves as others see you, though you might account yourselves spiritually true, you would know for a certainty that you were morally false. Little duties are almost too insignificant for such high-flying spiritual professors. They are brethren that can pray at a prayer-meeting, therefore they need not do an honest day's work for an honest day's wage. On the other hand, they can oppress the labourer in his wages because they mean to give a donation to the hospital. It will not do. In vain you pretend to be spiritual, and attend to spiritual duties, while you leave the commonplace morals in abeyance. Depend upon it, man, if you are not moral, you are not a disciple of Christ. It is all nonsense about your experience. If you occasionally get drunk, or if you now and then let fall an oath, or if in your business you would make twice two into five or three, according as your profit happens to run,—why, man, do not talk about being a Christian. Christ has nothing to do with you, at least no more to do with you than he had to do with

Judas Iscariot. You are very much in the same position. "Without holiness no man shall see the Lord." If without holiness, then much more without morality, can no man expect to see the face of God with acceptance. But, as true believers in our Lord, we do hope that he will enable us to have respect unto all God's commandments.

Some commandments specially concern the church. Every Christian should endeavour to discharge his duties towards his fellow Christians. There are also duties connected with the family, and every Christian should see that he does not let one of these kill the other. I did once know a man—I cannot tell you whether he is alive at this present moment—I knew him well; he used to go out into the villages with all the local preachers. He was a constant attendant at prayer-meetings —in fact, you never went to a public service connected with the church without seeing him—and he was out at tract society and missionary anniversaries, and every gathering of the sort; the only place where you never found him was at home with his boys. I had the misery to teach one of his boys. That boy died in drunkenness ere he had reached the age of manhood. Others of his sons were the pest of the town in which he lived. That man was eminently good in certain respects, doing a great deal for other people's families, but nothing for his own. Now, that will not do, brothers and sisters. That will never do. We must never bring to God as a sacrifice a duty smeared with the blood of another duty. That were an abomination. There is a balance and a proportion to be observed. "Then shall I not be ashamed, when I have respect unto all thy commandments."

The works of the Christian life may be divided, if you like, into public and private. How zealous some individuals are in the discharge of public work. Anything that will be seen of men shall have their closest attention. But how about private work? We attend the prayer-meeting, but do we forsake the closet? We hear sermons, but do we read our Bibles alone? We attend public meetings, but do we have private communion with God? O beloved, there are two sets of duties, the outward and the inward. What though to outward observation we walk uprightly before God, and there be nothing about us that the human eye can detect as wrong, yet if the heart be not pure, if though the outside of the platter is washed the inside is full of filthiness, how far we are from perfection! These reflections ought to cause a world of self-examination while I press home the crucial words—"Then shall I not be ashamed, when I have respect unto all thy commandments"—those divine injunctions which concern the secret inward life, as well as those which have to do with our more outward and public carriage.

We sometimes divide Christian duties into greater and smaller. Of course they are all great; none are small except in their bearing upon others, and some things do appear to have less relative magnitude. Now, some people are remiss and careless about what they call petty, trivial matters, but the genuine lover of the Lord will show his love to his Master in bestowing much care upon little things. I know it is in a family the little things that bring discomfort, and the little things that give pleasure; and I believe in the family of God those who give diligent heed to the little things of the word usually bring much comfort to their fellow Christians and great glory to God. At the same time, there were Pharisees of old who strained out gnats from their drink, but swallowed camels by their immoralities. There were those who tithed mint and anise and cummin, and yet neglected the weightier matters of the law. This must never occur with us. We must endeavour to have such a careful walk that we would not go an inch astray; and yet it is idle to talk about going an inch astray when we give ourselves license for a mile or two of wandering every now and then. God grant we may have grace to avoid small faults, while we strive to keep clear of great transgressions.

One other word I would like to say here. In the full sweep of our text there must be taken in duties unknown as well as known. "Then shall I not be ashamed, when I have respect unto all thy commandments." There may be some of God's commandments that you do not know. Study the word of God in order that you may know them. "Well," says one, "but I am excused if I do not know them." Do you really think so? because, if so, the more ignorant a man is the safer he is from coming into condemnation; for, knowing little, he is under little obligation, according to such an estimation. But our understanding and knowledge are not the measure of our duty. The command of God is our sole standard. Conscience itself is not a trustworthy rule. If a man's conscience be unenlightened, he may be sinning, and reaping the ill consequences of his sin, not less surely because he is not conscious that his misfortunes are due to his folly rather than his fate. His conscience cannot be the standard. The standard is the law of God. Brother, I would not have thee live in daily neglect of a divine command which I am persuaded thou wouldest obey if thou didst know it. Hide not thyself behind a pillar, but come into the light, and take the word and read it, and always ask that God would be pleased to open your eyes to anything there you have not hitherto seen. You know you can wink very hard sometimes when you are reading the Bible. I should say that our friends in the Southern states of America, when they kept slaves, must have winked dreadfully hard when they were reading such a passage as this: "As ye would that men should do to you, do ye also unto them likewise." And I could mention some other matters that concern English people, that would require a frequent putting the finger on the eye-ball, for fear too much light should come in. But be ye not such. Seek to let the word photograph itself upon your understanding, and then straightway when you know the divine will labour to carry it out in all particulars. Thus have I tried to show the range of this text.

But now notice that what is aimed at here is that the soul should pay respect unto all God's commandments—pay respect to them—love them, estimate them, value them, and thus pay respect to them all. I do not know whether you catch my thought, for I am afraid that I am putting it rather awkwardly. The commands of God are proportionate to one another. When an architect is about to erect a large edifice, say a cathedral, he has to make the height of the various proportions relative to each other. He grasps an idea of what the general effect is to be, so he does not throw out all his strength upon the nave, or the transept, or the chancel, or the spire, but he tries to make each part of the magnificent pile assist and contribute to the general harmony of the entire structure. Now, it ought to be just so with the Christian life. " Then shall I not be ashamed, when I have respect unto all thy commandments "—to the foundation commandments, striving to dig deep : to the high soaring commandments, seeking to rise into the utmost fellowship with God; to those commandments that need stern labour, like the rugged walls upon which much toil must be spent, and upon those which are a delight and a beauty, like the golden aureole windows that require fine taste and delicate skill. One would wish to do it all, to realize it all, to aim after a completeness of character, that we may be like to the Lord Jesus Christ. Oh that we were enamoured of this perfection, and were seeking after it ! It becomes us, dear friends, who are believers in Christ, to set before us as our standard a perfect character, and we should aim to reach it, looking to have the mind and will of God for that model. That I may in all things do what God requires of me, and abstain from everything which he forbids me, should be the great object of my life. Be it my firm resolve, and my daily and hourly desire, that, by the power of his Spirit, I may attain this conformity to the divine purpose. I should endeavour with constant maintained persistency to get nearer and nearer to this obedience to every divine commandment. Every failure should cost me sorrow. Every mistake should lead me to chasten myself with penitence. Every time I err I should go to the blood again and ask to be washed, that no defilement may remain upon me.

II. Having thus expatiated upon this universal obedience, only a few minutes can be afforded for the reward, to wit—THE EXCELLENCY OF ITS RESULT, " Then shall I not be ashamed."

I suppose that means, first, that as sin is removed, shame is removed. Sin and shame came into this world together. Our first parents were naked and were not ashamed, but when in another sense they became naked, then they were ashamed. They had no sooner sinned against God than they were told that they were naked, and they hid themselves from the presence of the Most High. Unless sin gets to a high head, which it will not do in the believer, shame is sure always to go with sin. Excessive sin or habitual transgression at last kills shame and gives a harlot's forehead, so that the hardened culprit knows not how to blush. It is an awful thing when a man is no longer conscious of shame, but a more awful thing still when he comes to glory in his shame ; for then his damnation is not far off. But as sin is cast out of the believer, shame is cast out of him in proportion, and it thence comes to pass that courage rises with a consciousness of rectitude. The man that has respect unto God's commands is no longer ashamed of men. He is not abashed by their scorn, or disconcerted by their ridicule. Let them say, " Oh, you are too precise." We should be very foolish to take that as a reproach. I remember once a man contemptuously calling me John Bunyan as I went down the street. I took off my hat to him, and felt rather flattered. I only wished I had been more like him. If anybody says to you, " Oh, you are a Methodist," take the imputation kindly. It is a most respectable name. Some of the grandest men that ever lived were Methodists. " Ah," but they will say, " you are one of the Presbyterians." Do not frown at the charge, but bow courteously; for some grand witnesses for Christ have belonged to that goodly fellowship. "Ah," says the world, "you are one of those Puritans—you are one of those religious people." Yes, but you are not ashamed of that. They might as well have said, "You are a man worth £50,000 a year." Would you blush to own it? I dare say you would like it to be true. When anybody says, "Ah, there is one of the saints," ask him to prove his words. Tell him you only hope you will try to prove them yourself. There is nothing to be ashamed of in keeping God's commands.

Then, again, before men we shall not be ashamed of our profession. Well may some Christians be inclined to put their Christianity into the shade when they recollect how little credit they do to it; but when a man has respect unto all God's commands, he is not ashamed to say, "I am a Christian. Look me up and down and examine my conduct. I do not boast of it, but I know that I have sought honestly and sincerely to walk before God in righteousness." Or, when an accusation is brought against you falsely, meet it in the same spirit. Mayhap somebody will libel you. I will defy you to avoid it. If you were to live the life of the most irreproachable man of God you would not be safe from calumny. Was not God himself slandered, even in Paradise, by the serpent? But you need not be ashamed when you can appeal to God and feel that in all things you have endeavoured to keep his commands. Thrice is he armed that has his conscience clear. No armour of steel or mail can so well protect a man as to know that before God he has walked in guileless, blameless uprightness, and sought to do before the Lord that which is well pleasing in his sight. "Then shall I not be ashamed, when I have respect unto all thy commandments."

This may likewise refer to that inward shame we sometimes feel when we examine ourselves, and pass our own conduct in review. Do not you ever, when reading a promise, look upon it as a very sweet promise made to God's children, though you hardly dare appropriate it to yourself? You feel ashamed. In fact, there are many gracious promises you never have yet been able to accept as your own. You have been afraid to take them. They were too rich, too ripe, too luscious fruit for you to adventure upon tasting: you thought they were intended for the favoured children, not for poor strangers like you. Now call to remembrance my text: "Then shall I not be ashamed, when I have respect unto all thy commandments." There are some delightful privileges of the Christian that you have never yet ventured to seek; some high doctrines that you have scarcely been able to believe. Dear friend, have respect unto all his commandments; for, perhaps, your fear, your doubt, your hesitancy, your want of assurance may have arisen from your want of a careful walk before God; and when the Holy Spirit has enabled you to be holy, he will enable you by full assurance to grasp the rich things of the covenant.

Now, may I not be speaking to some who have been ashamed of attempting their obvious duty. It is your duty to tell your experience sometimes to others, but you have blushed at the very thought. I know why. It was because you thought of some inconsistency which, if they knew, would disparage your testimony and make you appear very faulty in their eyes. Ah, "Then shall I not be ashamed, when I have respect unto all thy commandments." You have not dared to address even the smallest congregation yet though you can speak very well upon secular topics. Why is that? Is that because your walk is not as close with God as it should be? "Then shall I not be ashamed, when I have respect unto all thy commandments."

Perhaps, my brother, you may be a minister, and yet sometimes you may almost falter in stating some grand doctrinal truth. Why is that, brother? Is there something at the back that I cannot guess—that I would not mention if I could—which weakens your testimony? Yet you will not be ashamed when you have respect unto all God's commandments. How can we stand to admonish the unrighteous if we are not living righteous lives ourselves? How can we be able, like Nathan, to say, "Thou art the man," if we are conscious that the person rebuked could turn round and point at our lives and say, "See what you do." No, brethren, the servants of God that are to have courage in doing duty for their Master must pray to be the undefiled in the way, they must walk in the law of the Lord; and though at the very best, should they reach the highest point, they will still lie low before God and be humble in his presence, yet they will not be ashamed when they can feel that they have, in all integrity, walked before the Lord, and can say, like the prophet of old, "Whose ox have I taken? or whose ass have I taken? or whom have I defrauded? whom have I oppressed? or of whose hand have I received any bribe to blind mine eyes therewith? and I will restore it you. Witness against me before the Lord, and before his anointed." But if they could not impugn him, it gives the man grace not to be ashamed. So will it be in the time of trial, too. I admire Job, notwithstanding the testiness he seemed to have, and I wonder who would not be testy when he was covered with sore boils from head to foot: yet it was a grand thing to be able to say, "O God, thou knowest I am not wicked"; and he could appeal to the Eternal as his vindicator, because the charges brought against him were not true ; he had not sinned against his God in the way in which they said. Though he was not perfect in his nature, yet he was pure in heart; he was sincere in his disposition, and blameless in his outward carriage, so that he could defy them to prove any one of the insinuations that they hurled at his integrity. This helped him to triumph. It was the very backbone of his patience. And what satisfaction will it supply when our course is reaching its close, and we face the hour of our departure, if no dark clouds hang over our retrospect of life. Let God s grace enable you and me to live godly lives, we shall find then our evidences clear. Though we shall not ever rely upon any works of righteousness that we have achieved, or any character of holiness that we have acquired, but shall ever rest as much in Christ as we did when at first we cast our sinful souls on him for mercy, yet still it will be sweet to look back upon a life that has been spent in the service of God, and to exchange this service below for the nobler service of his courts above.

And when our course is finished, and we are gathered to our fathers, do you not think it will be well to leave an unclouded reputation behind? Did you ever notice the painful contrast between the record concerning one and another of the good kings of Judah? Take for example

Amaziah and Hezekiah. Of Amaziah it is said, " He did that which was right in the sight of the Lord, yet *not* like David his father. Howbeit the high places were not taken away : as yet the people did sacrifice and burnt incense on the high places." There was no such qualification to the tribute offered to Hezekiah's memory. " He did that which was right in the sight of the Lord, according to all that David his father did. He removed the high places, and brake the images, and cut down the groves, and brake in pieces the brazen serpent that Moses had made : for unto those days the children of Israel did burn incense to it : and he called it Nehushtan. He trusted in the Lord God of Israel ; so that after him was none like him among all the kings of Judah, nor any that were before him." So, brethren and sisters, I pray it may be with each and all of us, though we may not hold any such exalted position as the kings of Judah, yet let it be our desire and our aim to be " sincere and without offence till the day of Christ."

Once more, and I have done. "Then shall I not be ashamed, when I have respect unto all thy commandments."

" Then I shall not be ashamed before God." There is such a thing as a child of God being very much ashamed in the presence of his Father. He does not doubt that he is a child, but yet he feels ashamed. Is it not so with your own children ? They know that they are your children, and they know that you love them, but still they are ashamed, because they have been doing something which grieves you, and so they do not seek your company. They get away from father. Father has looked very angrily at them. And yet you never say, " Oh, you are not your father's child, because you have done wrong, and your father will turn you out of the family." They are never apprehensive of your casting them off. Oh no ; they are Calvinistic enough to know that they are not threatened with such a punishment, but at the same time they are fully aware—and it is enough to distress them—that their father is vexed, and that he frowns, so they keep out of his way. Now, remember, if we walk in the light as he is in the light, we have fellowship one with another, and " the blood of Jesus Christ his Son cleanses us from all sin." But we must walk in the light, or else we shall not have fellowship with God. Sin will mar and break up that fellowship. Sin will make thee leave off communing, or else communing will make thee leave off sinning. The two things are not consistent with each other. I, of course, mean not by sinning those sins of infirmity which we commit unconsciously, but I mean a general habit of sinning, to which our wilfulness or our negligence contribute. No rebellion or remissness can be tolerated in those who are living with God. Have you ever noticed two boys that want some indulgence, and one of them says, " Ask father for so-and-so. Ask father to let us have a holiday." The other says, "John, you ask him." " No," says John, " I cannot ask him, you ask him." " Why should the younger one ask ?" " Well," John says, " you know I have offended father, and though of course he loves me, yet I do not think it is quite the time for me to go and ask of him any great favour. You go and ask for us both." Have you not felt like that when engaged in prayer sometimes when you have not been walking with God as you should ? You could pray for forgiveness ; you could pray for common mercies ; but as for any great favour or special mercy, you have felt ashamed at such times to ask, and you have been glad for some brother to open his mouth a little wider than you dared, and ask for the church and you some great blessing. O Lord, thy servant knows what it is to draw near to thy mercy-seat, but he feels as if he was not on such terms with thee as usual, and that he cannot offer prayers and intercessions with that sense of liberty he has often enjoyed. There are other times when God meets us with the kisses of his love, and says, "Ask what thou wilt, and it shall be given to thee." It is grand praying with us then. "Then shall I not be ashamed, when I have respect unto all thy commandments." I shall not plead my obedience before thee. Nay, verily; but I shall plead the blood and righteousness of Christ, and this I shall do with all the greater boldness because my heart is sprinkled from an evil conscience : and that same Spirit which has wrought obedience in me will work in me the spirit of adoption, and he that taught me to listen to thy voice will teach me so to speak that thou wilt listen to my voice, and an answer of peace shall come to me. May God bless you, comfort your hearts, and stablish you in every good word and work, for Jesus's sake. Amen.

PORTION OF SCRIPTURE READ BEFORE SERMON—Psalm cxix. 1—16.

The Work of Grace
the Warrant for Obedience

" He that made me whole, the same said unto me, Take up thy bed and walk."—
John v. 11.

JUST a few observations upon the narrative itself. It was a feast day, and Jesus Christ came up to Jerusalem to find opportunities for doing good among the crowds of his countrymen. I see all the city glad; I hear the voice of rejoicing in every house as they hold high festival and eat the fat and drink the sweet. But where does Jesus keep the feast? How does he spend his holiday? He walks among the poor, whom he loves so well. Behold him in the hospital. There was one notable Bethesda or house of mercy in Jerusalem : it was a poor provision for the city's abounding sickness, but such as it was it was greatly prized. There was a pool which every now and then was stirred by an angel's wing, and wrought an occasional cure, and around it charitable persons had built five porches, and there on the cold stone steps a number of blind and halt and withered folk were lying, each one upon his own wretched pallet, waiting for the moving of the waters. There were the weary children of pain, fainting while others were feasting, racked with pain amid general rejoicing, sighing amid universal singing. Our Lord was at home amid this mercy, for here was room for his tender heart and powerful hand. He feasted his soul by doing good. Let us learn this lesson, dear friends, that in the times of our brightest joys we should remember the sorrowful, and find a still higher joy in doing them good. It well becomes us in proportion as a day is gladsome to ourselves to make it so to the sick and poor around us. Let us keep the feast by sending portions to those for whom nothing is prepared, for else the famishing may bring a curse upon our feasting. When we are prospered in business let us set aside a portion for the poor. When we are full of health and strength let us recollect those to whom these privileges are denied, and aid those who minister to them. Blessed shall they be who, like the Lord Jesus, visit the sick and care for t..em.

Coming into the hospital our Lord noticed a certain man whose case was a very sad one. There were many painful cases there, but he singled out this man, and it would seem that the reason for his choice was that the poor creature was in the worst plight of all. If misery has a claim on pity, then the greater the sufferer the more is mercy attracted towards him. This poor victim of rheumatism or paralysis had been thirty-eight years bound by his infirmity. Let us hope there was no worse case in all Bethesda's porches! Thirty-eight years is more than half the appointed period of human life. One year of pain or paralysis has a weary length of torture about it, but think of thirty-eight! We may well pity the man who endures the pangs of rheumatism even for an hour, but how shall we sufficiently pity him who has not been free from it for hard on forty years? Even if the case was not one of pain, but of paralysis, the inability to work and the consequent poverty of so many years were by no means a small evil. Our Lord, then, selects the worst case to be dealt with by his curing hand, as a type of what he often does in the kingdom of grace, and as a lesson of prudence to us, instructing us to give our first aid to those who are first in point of need.

The man whom Jesus healed was by no means an attractive character. Our Saviour said to him when he was healed, "Sin no more, lest a worse thing come unto thee," from which it is not an improbable inference that his first infirmity had come upon him by some deed of vice or course of excess. In some way or other he had been guilty of that which brought upon his body the suffering which he was enduring. Now, it is considered generally to be a point beyond all dispute that we should help the worthy but should refuse the worthless,—that when a man brings a calamity upon himself by wrong doing we are justified in letting him suffer, that he may reap what he has sown. This cold Pharisaic idea is very congenial to minds which are bent upon saving their coin. It springs up in many hearts, or rather in places where hearts ought to be, and it is generally regarded as if it were a rule of prudence which it would be sinful to dispute, an axiom infallible and universal. Now, I venture to say that our Saviour never taught us to confine our alms to the deserving. He would never have bestowed the grand alms of grace on any one of us if he had carried out that rule ; and if you and I had received no more at the hands of God than we deserved, we should not have been in this house of prayer. We cannot afford to cramp our charity into a sort of petty justice, and sour our almsgiving into a miniature assizes. When a man is suffering let us pity him, however the suffering has come. When a man had been in misery so long as thirty-eight years, it was time that his infirmity should be more considered than his iniquity, and that his present sorrow should be thought upon more than his former folly. So Jesus thought, and therefore he came to the sinner, not with reproach, but with restoration ; he saw his disease rather than his depravity, and gave him pity instead of punishment. Our God is kind to the unthankful and to the evil; be ye therefore merciful, as your Father also is merciful. Remember how our Lord said, " Pray for them that despitefully use you, that you may be the children of your Father which is in heaven ; for he maketh his sun to rise on the evil and on the good, and sendeth rain on the just and on the unjust." Let us imitate him in this, and wherever there is pain and sorrow let it be our joy to relieve it.

In addition to the supposition that this man had at some time been grossly guilty, it seems pretty clear from the text that he was a poor, shiftless, discouraged, inanimate, stupid sort of body. He had never managed to get into the pool, though others had done so who were as infirm as himself. He had never been able to win a friend or secure a helper, though from the extreme length of his infirmity one would have thought that at some period or another he might have found a man to place him in the pool when the angel gave it the mystic stir. The Saviour's asking him, "Wilt thou be made whole?" leads us to think that he had fallen into such a listless, despairing, heart-sick condition, that though he came daily to the edge of the pool as a matter of habit, he had not only ceased to hope, but had almost ceased to wish. Our Lord touched the chord which was most likely to respond, namely, his will and desire to be made whole, but the response was a very feeble one. His answer shows what a poor creature he was, for there is not a beam of hope in it, or even of desire : it is a wail, a hopeless dirge, a grievous complaint: "I have no man, when the water is troubled, to put me into the pool : but while I am coming, another steppeth down before me." But the utter imbecility and want of brain of the poor creature is most seen in the fact that like a simpleton he went to Christ's enemies and told them that it was Jesus that had made him whole. I am sure there was no malice in his thus informing our Lord's enemies, for if there had been he would have said, "It was Jesus who bade me take up my bed," whereas he worded it thus, "It was Jesus which had made him whole." I hardly dare, however, to hope, as some do, that there was much gratitude about this testimony, though doubtless the poor soul was grateful; I conceive that his long endurance of pain, acting upon a weak mind, had brought him to an almost imbecile state of mind, so that he spoke without thought. Our Lord did not, therefore, require much of him, he did not ask even for a distinct avowal of faith from him, but only for that small measure of it which might be implied in his answering the question, "Wilt thou be made whole?" This poor man evinced none of the shrewdness of the man born blind, who answered the Pharisees so keenly ; he was of quite another type, and could do no more than state his own case to Jesus. Thank God, even that was enough for our Lord to work with. The Lord Jesus saves people of all sorts. He hath among his disciples men of quick and ready wit, who can baffle their opponents, but quite as often

> " He takes the fool and makes him know
> The wonders of his dying love :
> To bring aspiring wisdom low,
> And all its pride reprove."

So here he chose this poor simpleton of a creature and wrought a great marvel upon him, to the exceeding praise of his condescending grace.

Note well that this man's mind, though there was not much of it, was all engrossed and filled up with the fact that he had been made whole. Jesus to him was " he that made me whole." Of the person of Jesus he knew next to nothing, for he had only seen him for an instant, and then he wist not that it was Jesus : his one idea of Jesus was, " He that made me whole." Now, beloved brethren, this was natural in his case, and it will be equally natural in our own. Even when the saved ones are more intelligent, and of larger mind than this poor paralytic, they must still chiefly think of the Son of God as their Saviour, as he that made them whole. If I do not know much about the Lord, yet I do know that he has saved me. I was burdened with guilt and full of woes, and could not rest day nor night until he gave me peace. If I cannot tell another much concerning the glory of his person, his attributes, his relationships, his offices, or his work, yet I can say "one thing I know, whereas I was blinded by error, now I see; whereas I was paralyzed by sin, I am now able to stand upright and walk in his ways." This poor soul knew the Lord experimentally, and that is the best way of knowing him. Actual contact with him yields a surer knowledge, and a truer knowledge, than all the reading in the world. In the kingdom of Christ wonderful facts transpire, such as conversion and finding peace with God; and happy are they to whom these facts are personal experiences. When men are turned from the error of their ways, and when their heart finds rest and peace in Christ great deeds are done by the Lord Jesus; and if you are acquainted with these two things, even though you should be ignorant of a great deal else, be not afraid of exaggerating their importance, but set your mind on them, and call Jesus by that name,—"He that made me whole." Think of him under that aspect, and you will have a very valuable and influential idea of him. You shall see greater things than these, but for the present let these happy and sure facts be much upon your mind, even as his being made whole was upon this man's mind.

As for the cavilling Pharisees, you observe that they took no notice of the glorious fact of the man's cure; they wilfully ignored what Christ had done, but they fell full swoop upon that little, insignificant circumstance that it had been done on the Sabbath-day, and then they spent all their thoughts and emotions upon that side issue. They say nothing of the man's being restored, but they rage because he carried his bed on the Sabbath-day. It is much the same with the men of the world at this day. They habitually ignore the fact of conversion; if they do not deny it they look upon it as being a trifle, a matter not worth caring about. What though they see the harlot made chaste, and the thief made honest, and the profane made devout, and the despairing made joyful, and other moral and spiritual changes of the utmost practical value, they forget all this, and they attack some peculiar point of doctrine, or mode of speech, or diversity of manner, and raise a storm concerning these. Is it because the facts themselves, if fairly looked at, would establish what they do not care to believe? The fact that Christianity is doing marvels in the world, such as nothing else ever did, they persistently forget, but that fact is just what you and I must as persistently remember. We must dwell upon what Christ has by his Holy Spirit wrought within our nature by renewing us in the spirit of our minds, and we must make this work of grace a fountain of argument which shall establish our faith and justify our conduct. This poor man did so. He did not know much else, but that he had been made whole he did know, and from that fact he justified himself in what he had done. "He that made me whole, the same said unto me, take up thy bed and walk."

This is the truth which I want to enlarge upon this morning—first, by saying that the work of Christ furnishes us with *a justification for our obedience to his command*—" He that made me whole, the same said to me"—that is our complete justification for what we do. In the second place, the work of Jesus Christ throws upon us *an obligation to do what he bids us*—if he that made me whole says to me, take up thy bed and walk, I am bound to do it, and I ought to feel the obligation of his goodness pressing upon me; and, in the third place, it is not only a justification and an obligation, but the deed of grace becomes a *constraint to obedience*—he that said unto me, "rise," and so made me whole, by that same word of power made me take up my bed and walk. The power which saves us also moves us to obey our Saviour. Not with our own might do we fulfil the will of our Lord, but with power which the Healer gives us in the self-same hour. You see the drift, therefore, of our discourse. May the Holy Spirit lead us into the power of this truth, for I am persuaded that a sense of the Lord's work within us is a great force, and should be excited and applied to the highest ends.

I. First, then, this is our JUSTIFICATION for what we do when we obey Christ. This poor man could not defend the action of taking up his bed and walking, for his enemies were learned in the law and he was not. You and I could defend it very easily, for it seems to us a very proper thing to do under the circumstances. The weight of his bed was not much more than that of an ordinary great coat, it was a simple rug or mat upon which he was lying; there really was no violation of God's law of the Sabbath, and therefore there was nothing to excuse. But the Rabbis laid down rules of which I will give you but one specimen—"It is unlawful to carry a handkerchief loose in the pocket;" but if you pin it to your pocket or tie it round your waist as a girdle you may carry it anywhere, because it becomes a part of your dress. To my unsophisticated mind it would have seemed that the pin increased the ponderous burden, and that so there was the weight of the pin more than was necessary! This was quite a weighty business according to Rabbinical estimates. The most of the Rabbinical regulations with regard to the Sabbath were absolutely ludicrous, but this poor man was not in a position to say so or even to think so, for, like the rest of his countrymen, he stood in awe of the scribes and doctors. These learned ·pharisees and priests were too much reverenced for this poor creature to answer them in their own manner; but he did what you and I must always do when we are at all puzzled;—he hid behind the Lord Jesus, and pleaded, "He that made me whole, the same said unto me, take up thy bed." That was quite enough for him, and he quoted it as if he felt that it ought to be enough for those who questioned him. Truly it ought to have been so. I may not be able to find in my own knowledge and ability an authority equal to the authority of learned unbelievers, but my personal experience of the power of grace will stand me in as good a stead as this man's cure was to him. He argued that there must be in the man who made him whole enough authority to match the greatest possible rabbi that ever lived. Even his poor, feeble mind could grasp that, and surely you and I may do the same, we can defend ourselves behind the breastwork of our Saviour's gracious work, and the consequent authority which belongs to him.

There are certain *ordinances* to which a Christian man is bound to attend, about which the world raises a storm of questions. The world does not take notice that this man was once a drunkard and has through divine grace become sober, and so has become a good father, and a good husband, and a good citizen. It lets that miracle pass by unheeded, but he is going to be baptized, and they at once object to the ordinance, or he is going to join a Christian church, and straightway they jeer at him as a Presbyterian, or a Methodist, as if it matters what sort of name they give him so long as he is a better man than themselves, and is redeemed from sin, and taught to be upright, and chaste, and pure in the sight of God. The work of grace goes for nothing with them, but just the peculiarity of sect, or the peculiarity of religious rite is made a world of. Blind creatures to despise the medicine which heals because of the bottle which contains it, or the label by which it is named. However, our answer is, "He that made us whole," the same gave us a command, and by that command we will abide. We seek no justification but this, that he who wrought a miracle of grace upon us bade us do it. What if I am about to be baptized as a believer, the same that said "Believe" said "Be baptized": he who gave me salvation the same said, "He that believeth, and is baptized, shall be saved." Over against all objections we set the divine authority of Jesus. He by whose blood we are cleansed, and by whose Spirit we are renewed, is Lord and lawgiver to us. His precept is our sufficient warrant. If we go to the communion table, and revilers say, "What is the use of eating a piece of bread and drinking a drop of wine? Why think so solemnly of so small a matter?" We reply, He that made us whole, the same said, "Do this in remembrance of me." We abjure what he has not ordained, but we cling to his statutes. If he had commanded a rite still more trivial, or a ceremony still more open to objection in the eyes of carnal man, we would make no further apology than this :—He who has created us anew, and given us a hope of heaven, and led us to seek after perfect holiness—he has bidden us do it. This is our final reply, and although we could find other justifications they would be superfluous. Stand that for our defence—the Saviour commands.

The same apology applies to all *the doctrines* of the gospel. I say again, ungodly men will not admit. or if they admit it they ignore it, that the gospel works a marvellous change in men's hearts. If they want proof we can find them instances by hundreds, and by thousands, of the reclaiming, elevating, and purifying power of the gospel of Jesus Christ. The gospel is daily working spiritual miracles, but this they forget, and they go on to find fault with its peculiar doctrines. Justification by faith they frequently quarrel with. "Well now," they say, "that is a shocking doctrine : if you teach men that they are to be saved by faith alone, and not by their works, of course they will lead loose lives ; if you continually declare that salvation is of grace alone, and not of merit, the inevitable result will be that men will sin that grace may abound." We find a complete answer to this calumny in the fact that believers in justification by faith and in the doctrines of grace are among the best and purest of men, and that as a fact these truths work holiness ; but we do not care to argue thus ; we prefer to remind our adversaries that he who has caused us to be regenerate men himself taught us that whosoever believeth in him shall be saved, and expressly declared that he that believeth in him hath everlasting life. By the mouth of his servant

Paul he has said that by grace are men saved through faith, and that not of themselves, it is the gift of God. He hath also told us that by the works of the law shall no flesh be justified, and he has bidden us declare that "the just shall live by faith." He who is daily by his gospel turning men from sin to holiness has given this for the sum total of the gospel we are to preach—"Look unto me, and be ye saved, all the ends of the earth." If this gospel does not make men better, and change their evil natures, you may question it if you like, and we do not wonder that you should; but while it continues its purifying work we shall not blush or stammer when we declare the doctrines which are its essence and life. Our regeneration proves to us our Lord's authority, and upon that we are prepared to base our creed. To us the best of evidence is his work within us, and in that evidence we place implicit faith.

The same applies also to all *the precepts* which the Christian is called upon to obey. For instance, if he is true to his colours, he keeps himself aloof from all the sinful pleasures, practices, and policies of the world, in which others take delight, and consequently the ungodly world says that he is singular, precise, and self-opinionated. This is the answer for all Christians—"He that made us whole, the same said to us, ye are not of the world, even as I am not of the world. Come ye out from among them and be ye separate, touch not the unclean thing, and I will receive you." If you follow the precepts of the Lord Jesus Christ you may meet all charges of singularity by urging the supremacy of the Saviour, whose power has made you a new creature. Where his word is, there is a power to which we bow at once. It is not ours to question our Saviour, but to obey him. We are cleansed by his blood, we are redeemed by his death, and we live by his life, and therefore are not ashamed to take up his cross and follow him.

This apology ought to suffice even those who oppose us, for if they felt as grateful as we do they would obey also. They ought at any rate to say, "We cannot blame these men for doing as Jesus bids them, because he has done so much for them." Surely the poor man who had been thirty-eight years paralyzed could not be blamed for obeying the command of one who in a moment restored him to health and strength. If he became his servant for life, who would censure him? Who would say that he too tamely submitted? Should not such a benefactor exert a boundless influence over him? What could be more natural and proper? Now, you unconverted people must excuse us, if we, in obedience to our Lord Jesus, do many things which to you seem very singular, for though we would not needlessly offend, we cannot please you at the risk of displeasing our Lord. We do not owe so much to you as we owe to him. We do not owe so much to the whole world as we owe to the Lord Jesus; in fact, truth to tell, we do not feel that we owe anything to the world. The time past sufficeth us to have wrought the will of the Gentiles, for when we are asked the question, "What fruit had ye then in those things whereof ye are now ashamed?" we have to confess that we had no fruit, except the sour grapes, which have set our teeth on edge. Like the shipmen who put out to sea against Paul's advice, our only gain has been loss and damage. In serving the world we found the labour weariness and the wages death; but as for our Lord

Jesus, we owe him everything, and so you must excuse us if we try to follow him in everything. It seems to us that this is an excuse which you ought to accept from us as covering the whole ground, but if you refuse it we are not at all dismayed, for it quite suffices *us*, yea, more than suffices us, it makes us glory in what we do. Does Jesus command? Then it is ours to obey. Objectors may say concerning one of his ordinances, it is unsuitable to the climate, it is indecent, it is needless, it is I do not know what: all this is no concern of ours, if Jesus bade us do it, his command stands for us in the place of reasoning. He who made us whole gives us sufficient excuse for obedience in that very fact. " Oh, but it is contrary to what the fathers teach, and to what the church teaches." We care not the snap of our finger for all the fathers and all the churches under heaven if they go contrary to what our Lord teaches, for they did not make us whole, and we are not under obligation to them as we are to him. The authority of Jesus is supreme, because it is from his lips that we received the word which healed the sickness of our sin. This satisfies our conscience now, and it will do so amid the solemnities of death. How can we make a mistake if we follow the words of Jesus in all things? My brethren, we· can plead his precept as our warrant at the last great day, before the Judge of quick and dead. What better plea can we have than this, " Thou didst make us whole and thou didst bid us do this "? Such a justification of our conduct will make our death pillow soft and our resurrection bright with joy.

Instead of admitting that this is not an ample justification, let us go further still in the strength of it. If the world has accounted us vile for obeying our Lord, let us be viler still; and inasmuch as he that made us whole said, " Go ye into all the world and preach the gospel to every creature," let us endeavour to spread abroad everywhere the savour of his name, consecrating ourselves body, soul, and spirit to the extension of his kingdom. He who made us whole will make the world whole yet by his own wondrous power. Have we not abundantly shown that our Lord's command is a solid justification of our conduct?

II. And now, secondly, the cure brought forth AN OBLIGATION :—"He that made me whole, the same said unto me, Take up thy bed, and walk." The argument takes this form : first, if he made me whole he is divine, or he could not do this miracle; or, to say the least, he must be divinely authorised : and if he be divine, or divinely authorised, I must be bound to obey the orders which he issues. Is not that a plain argument which even the poor, simple mind of the paralytic man was able to grasp and wield? Let us try and feel the force of that argument ourselves. Jesus who has saved us is our God ; shall we not obey him ? Since he is clothed with divine power, and majesty, shall we not scrupulously endeavour to know his will, and zealously endeavour to carry it out in every point, as his Spirit shall enable us ?

In addition to the divine character which the miracle proved and displayed, there was the goodness which shone in the deed of power and touched the poor man's heart. His argument was—" I *must* do what my great Deliverer bids me. How can you think otherwise ? Did he not make me whole ? Would you have *me*, whom he has thus graciously restored, refuse to fulfil his desire ? Must I not take up my bed the moment he gives me strength to do it? How can I do otherwise? Is this to be the recompense I pay to my good Physician, at once to refuse to do what he asks of me? Do you not see that I am under an obligation which it would be shameful to deny? He restores these limbs, and I am bound to do with them what he orders me do with them. He says 'walk,' and since these once withered feet have been restored, shall I not walk? He bids me roll up my bed, and since I could not have used my hands till just now his word gave them life, shall I not use them to roll up the bed-rug at his bidding? These poor shoulders of mine were bent with weakness, but he has made me stand upright, and since he now bids me carry my bed, shall I not throw the mattress on my shoulders, and bear the easy load which he lays upon me?" There was no answering such reasoning. Whatever might have been the claim of Jesus upon others, he clearly had an indisputable right to the loyal obedience of one whom he had made perfectly whole.

Follow me briefly in this, brothers and sisters. If you have been saved by the grace of God, your salvation has put you under obligation henceforth to do what Jesus bids you. Are you redeemed? Then ye are not your own, ye are bought with a price. Have you been in consequence of what the Lord has done for you rescued from Satanic slavery and adopted into the divine family? Then it clearly follows that, because you are sons, you should be obedient to the law of the household; for is not this a first element of sonship, that you should reverence the great Father of the family? The Lord has been pleased to put away your sin, you are forgiven: but does not pardon demand amendment? Shall we go back to the old sins from which we have been cleansed? Shall we live in the iniquities from which we have been washed by the blood of our Lord Jesus? That were horrible to think of. It would be nothing less than devilish for a man to say, " I have been forgiven, and therefore I will sin again." There is no remission where there is no repentance. The guilt of sin remains on that man in whom the love of sin still remains. Let us practically feel the force of this, and follow after purity and righteousness henceforth.

Brethren and sisters upon whom Christ has wrought his great work, you have experienced the love of God, and therefore, if God has so loved you, you are bound to love him in return. If God has so loved you, you must also love your brother man? Do not love to God and love to man spring up as a sure consequence of the love of God shed abroad in the heart? Does not every one see the necessity which calls for the one love to follow the other? But love is the mother of obedience: thus everything connected with our Lord lays us under obligation to obey him. There is not a single blessing of the covenant but what necessarily entails its corresponding duty; and here I scarcely like to say *duty*, for these blessings of the covenant make duty to be our privilege and holiness to be our delight. Henceforth redeemed from sin we would live no longer therein: henceforth made heirs of heaven we endeavour to lead the heavenly life, so that even while we are below our conversation may be in heaven, from whence we look for the Saviour, the Lord Jesus Christ. Brethren, he that made you whole has commanded this and that to be done by you: I counsel you to keep the King's commandment. As Mary said to the waiters at the wedding at Cana so say I to you—" Whatsoever he saith unto you, do it." Doth he bid you pray, then pray without ceasing. Doth he bid you watch as well as pray, then guard every act, and thought, and word. Doth he bid you love your brethren? Then love them with a pure heart fervently. Doth he bid you serve them and humble yourself for his sake? Then do so, and become the servant of all. Hath he said, "Be ye holy, for I am holy"? Then aim at this by his Holy Spirit. Hath he said, "Be ye perfect, even as your Father which is in heaven is perfect?" Then strive after perfection, for he that made you whole has a right to direct your way, and it will be both your safety and your happiness to submit yourselves to his commands.

III. Enough, however, upon that; for now we call your attention, in the third place, to the text under the sense of CONSTRAINT—"He that made me whole, the same said unto me, take up thy bed and walk." He made him whole by saying, "Rise, take up thy bed." The carrying of the bed was part and parcel of the cure. The first part of the healing word was "rise," but the second was "take up thy bed." Now, it was not an ordinary word which Jesus spoke to that man—a mere word of advice, warning, or command; but it was a word full of power, like that which created light out of darkness. When the Lord said to the poor man, "Rise," he did rise. A thrill went through him; those stagnant blood vessels felt the life-blood stir and flow, those dormant nerves were aroused to sensations of health, those withered sinews and muscles braced themselves for energetic action, for omnipotence had visited the impotent man and restored him. Oh it must have been a wondrous joy to the long enervated, nerveless, powerless frame to be capable of healthy motion, to be equal to bearing a happy burden. The joyful man rolled up his bed, threw it on his back, and marched abroad with the best of them. The bed-carrying was part of the cure, and proof of the cure. The paralytic man had not been called upon to deliberate as to whether he should rise or not, but Jesus said, "Rise," and he stood upright: the same word said, "Take up thy bed," the bed was up at once, and according to the last word "walk," the man walked with delight. It was all done by the power of the one thrilling sentence, which tarried not to be questioned, but accomplished the end for which the Lord had sent it. Not unwillingly did the restored man carry his bed, yet he did it of constraint, for the same power which made him whole made him obedient. Before the divine energy had touched him, he seemed scarcely to have any will at all, and the Lord had to hunt to find a will in him, saying, "Wilt thou be made whole?" But now he cheerfully wills obedience to his benefactor, and in the force of the command he carried out the Lord's behest. I say that his taking up his bed, and walking, was done by Christ's enabling, and done by Christ's constraining, and I pray that you may know by experience what this means. What I want you to feel is this—"I cannot help obeying Christ, for by his Holy Spirit he has spoken me into a life which will never die and never be vanquished. He has spoken a word in me which has a continuous force over me, and thrills me through and through continually. I can no more help seeking to obey Christ than this man could help carrying his bed when the Lord, by a word of power, had bidden him do so."

Brethren, look at this, and be instructed and warned. Do you feel reluctant this morning to enter upon your Lord's service, because of conscious weakness? Has the devil tempted you to draw back from obedience, because of your unfitness? Do you hesitate? do you tremble? Surely you need to draw near to the Lord again, and hear his voice anew. Take your Bibles and let him speak to you again out of the word, and may the same thrill which awoke you out of your death-sleep wake you out of your present lethargy. There is need that the living word of God should come home to your inmost soul again with that same miraculous power which dwelt in it at first. "Lord, quicken thou me," is David's prayer, but it suits me every day, and I think the most of God's people would do well to use it daily. "Lord, speak life unto me now as thou didst at first. Speak power, speak spiritual force into me." "The love of Christ constraineth us," says the apostle : this constraint is what we want to feel more and more. We need divine life perpetually to bear us forward to acts of obedience. We do not want to destroy willinghood, but we would have it quickened into entire subservience to the will of the Lord. Like Noah's ark on dry land, the will keeps its place by its own dead weight ; O for a flood of grace to move, to lift, to upbear it ; to carry it away by a mighty current. We would be borne before the love of Christ as a tiny piece of wood is drifted by the gulf-stream, or as one of the specks which dance in the sunbeam would be carried by a rushing wind. As the impulse which began with Jesus found the poor man passive because utterly unable to be otherwise, and then impelled him on to active movements as with a rush of power, so may it ever be with us throughout life. May we for ever yield to the divine impulse. To be passive in the Lord's hands is a good desire, but to be what I would call actively passive, to be cheerfully submissive, willingly to give up our will, this is a higher spiritual mood. We must live, and yet not we, but Christ in us. We must act, and yet we must say, He that made me whole bade me do this holy deed, and I do it because his power moves me thereunto. If I have done well I lay the honour at his feet : if I hope to do well in the future it is because I hope for strength from him to do well, believing that he will work in me by that same power which converted me at the first. Beloved, endeavour to abide under this influence. May the Holy Spirit bring you there!

My last word is a practical lesson. The church of God on earth at this present time anxiously desires to spread her influence over the world. For Christ's sake we wish to have the truths we preach acknowledged, and the precepts which we deliver obeyed. But mark, no church will ever have power over the masses of this or any other land, except in proportion as she does them good. The day has long since passed in which any church may hope to prevail on the plea of history. "Look at what we were," is a vain appeal : men only care for what we are. The sect which glorifies itself with the faded laurels of past centuries, and is content to be inactive to-day, is near to its inglorious end. In the race of usefulness men nowadays care less about the pedigree of the horse and more about the rate at which it can run. The history of a congregation or a sect is of small account compared with the practical good which it is doing. Now, if any church under heaven can show that it is making men honest, temperate, pure, moral, holy, that it is seeking out the ignorant and instructing them, that it is seeking out the fallen and reclaiming them, that in fact it is turning moral wastes into gardens, and taking the weeds and briars of the wilderness and transforming them into precious fruit-bearing trees, then the world will be ready to hear its claims and consider them. If a church cannot prove its usefulness, the source of its moral strength will have gone, and, indeed, something worse than this will have happened, for its spiritual strength will have gone too ; for a barren church is manifestly without the fruitful Spirit of God. Brethren, you may, if you will, dignify your minister by the name of bishop, you may give to your deacons and elders grand official titles, you may call your place of worship a cathedral, you may worship if you will with all the grandeur of pompous ceremonial and the adornments of music and incense and the like, but you shall have only the semblance of power over human minds unless you have something more than these. But if you have a church, no matter by what name it is called, that is devout, that is holy, that is living unto God, that does good in its neighbourhood, that by the lives of its members spreads holiness and righteousness ; in a word, if you have a church that is really making the world whole in the name of Jesus, you shall in the long run find that even the most carnal and thoughtless will say, "The church which is doing this good is worthy of respect, therefore let us hear what it has to say." Living usefulness will not screen us from persecution, but it will save us from contempt. A holy church goes with authority to the world in the name of Jesus Christ its Lord, and this force the Holy Spirit uses to bring human hearts into subjection to the truth. Oh, that the church of God would believe in Jesus' power to heal sick souls. Recollect this man, thirty-eight years sick, had been longer ill than Christ had lived on earth. He had been seven years afflicted before Christ was born. And even so this poor world has been long afflicted. Years before the Pentecost, or the birth of the present visible church, the poor sinful world lay at the pool, and could not stir. We must not be hopeless about it, for yet the Lord will cast sin out of it. Let us go in Jesus Christ's name and proclaim the everlasting gospel, and say, " Rise, take up thy bed, and walk," and it shall be done, and God shall be glorified and we shall be blessed.

PORTION OF SCRIPTURE READ BEFORE SERMON—John v. 1—23.

The Withered Hand

"And, behold, there was a man which had his hand withered . . . . Then saith he to the man, Stretch forth thine hand. And he stretched it forth; and it was restored whole, like as the other."—Matthew xii. 10, 13.

NOTE well the expression. Jesus "went into their synagogue; and, *behold*, there was a man which had his hand withered." A mark is set, as it were, in the margin, as if it were a notable fact. That word "*behold*" is a sort of note of exclamation to draw attention to it. "Behold, there was a man which had his hand withered." In many congregations, if there should step in some one of the great and mighty of the land, people would say, "Behold, there was a duke, an earl, or a bishop there." But although there were some great ones occasionally in our Saviour's congregation, I find no notes of admiration about their presence, no "beholds" inserted by the evangelists as if to call attention to their appearance. No doubt if there were in a congregation some person of known intelligence and great learning, who had earned to himself a high degree, there are persons who would say, "Do you know that Professor Science or Doctor Classic was present at the service?" There would be a "behold" put to that in the memories of many. There were persons well learned, according to the learning of the day, who came to listen to Christ, but there are no "*beholds*" put about their having been present. Yet in the synagogue there was a poor man whose hand had been withered, and we are called upon to note the fact.

It was his *right* hand which was withered, the worse of the two for him, for he could scarcely follow his handicraft or earn his bread. His best hand was useless, his bread-winner failed him. I have no doubt he was a very humble, obscure, insignificant individual, probably very badly off and in great poverty, because he could not work as his fellow craftsmen could, but not a man of any rank, or learning, or special intelligence. His being in the assembly was in itself nothing very remarkable. I suppose he had been accustomed to go to the synagogue as others of his townsmen did; yet the Holy Spirit takes care to mark that he was present, and to have the word "behold" hung out like a signal, that it might be regarded as a special subject for consideration that the crippled man was there.

And to-night, dear friends, it matters very little to the preacher or to the congregation that *you* are here, if you are some person of note or consequence ; for we make no note of dignitaries here, and attach no special consequence to any one in this place, where the rich and the poor meet together. But if you happen to be here as a needy soul wanting a Saviour, if you happen to be here with a spiritually withered hand so that you cannot do the things that you would, and you are wanting to have that hand restored to you, there shall be a "*behold*" put to that, and especially shall it be doubly emphatic if to-night the Master shall say to you, "Stretch out thy withered hand," and if the divine power shall restore that hand and a deed of grace shall be accomplished. What our Lord wanted on that particular Sabbath morning was somebody to work upon, somebody whom he might heal, and so defy the traditional legality of the Pharisees who said that it was wrong to heal on the Sabbath day. Christ did not want their health that morning : he looked out for their sickness that he might illustrate his healing power. He did not want any greatness in anybody there ; but he did want some poor needy one in whom he could display his power to heal. And that is just the case to-night. If you are rich and increased in goods and have need of nothing, my Master does not want you. He is a physician, and those who practise the healing art look out for sickness as their sphere of operation. If we were to tell a wise physician of a town where nobody was sick, but everybody enjoyed perfect health, he would not settle there, unless he wished to retire from practice. My Master does not come into the assemblies where all feel themselves quite content with themselves, where there are no blind eyes, no deaf ears, no broken hearts, no withered hands; for what do such folks need with a Saviour? He looks around and his eye fixes itself upon pain, upon necessity, upon incapacity, upon sinfulness, upon everything to which he can do good ; for what he wants in us mortals is the opportunity to do us good and not a pretence on our part that we can do him good.

I begin with this, because my talk to-night will be very simple, and it will only be meant for those of you who want my Lord and Master. Those of you who do not need him can go ; but you that want him, it may be you shall find him to-night; and there shall be the record kept in heaven, not of those who were here, who said, "We see," nor of those who said, "Our hand is strong and deft for labour," but there shall be a register of blind ones who shall say, "Thou Son of David, open our eyes," and of withered ones who shall to-night stretch out their withered hands in obedience to his divine command. I do not know that our crippled friend when he went to the synagogue that morning expected to get his withered hand healed. Being, perhaps, a devout man, he went there to worship, but he got more than he went for. And it may be that some of you whom God means to bless to-night do not know what you have come here for. You came because you somehow love the ordinances of God's house, and you feel happy in hearing the gospel preached. You have never yet laid hold of the gospel for yourselves, never enjoyed its privileges and blessings as your own, but still you have a hankering after the best things. What if to-night the hour has come, the hour which sovereign grace has marked with a red letter in the calendar of love, in which your withered hand shall be made strong, and your sin shall be forgiven! What bliss if you shall go your way to glorify God because a notable miracle of grace has been wrought in you! God grant it may be so done by the power of the Holy Spirit. I entreat those of you who love the Master to pray him to work wonders at this time upon many, and his shall be the praise.

I. First, we will say a little about THE PERSON TO WHOM THE COMMAND IN OUR TEXT IS ADDRESSED. "Then said Jesus to the man, stretch forth thine hand."

This command was addressed, then, to *a man who was hopelessly incapable of obeying.* "Stretch forth thine hand." I do not know whether his arm was paralysed, or only his hand. As a general rule when a thorough paralysis, not a partial one, takes place in the hand it seizes the entire member, and both hand and arm are paralyzed. We usually speak of this man as if the entire limb had been dried up, and yet I do not see either in Matthew, Mark, or Luke, any express declaration that the whole arm was withered. It seems to me to have been a case in which the hand only was affected. We used to have, not far from here, I remember, at Kennington Gate, a lad who would frequently get on the step of the omnibus and exhibit his hands, which hung down as if his wrists were broken, and he would cry, "Poor boy! poor boy!" and appeal to our compassion. I fancy that his case was a picture of the one before us, in which, not the arm perhaps, but the hand had become dried up. We cannot decide positively that the arm was still unwithered, but we may notice that our Lord did not say, "Stretch out thy arm," but "thine hand," so that he points to the hand as the place where the paralysis lay. If he had said, "Stretch out thy arm," as the text does not declare that the arm was dried up, we should have said that Christ bade him do exactly what he was capable of doing, and there would have been no miracle in it. But inasmuch as he says, "Stretch forth thine hand," it is clear that the mischief was in the hand, if not in the arm; and so it was putting him to do what he could not possibly do, for the man's hand was assuredly withered. It was not a sham disease. He had not made a pretence of being paralyzed, but he was really incapable. The hand had lost the moisture of life. The spirits which gave it strength had been dried out of it, and there it was a withered, wilted, useless thing, with which he could do nothing; and yet it was to such a man that Jesus said, "Stretch forth thine hand."

This is very important for us to notice, because some of you under a burden of sin think that Christ does not save real sinners—that those people whom he does save are, in some respects, not quite so bad as you—that there is not such an intensity of sin about them as about your case, or if an intensity of sin, yet not such an utter hopelessness and helplessness as there is about you. You feel quite dried up, and utterly without strength. Dear hearer, it is exactly to such as you that the Lord Jesus Christ directs the commands of the gospel. We are bidden to preach to you, saying, "Believe," or at other times, "Repent, and be baptized, every one of you;" "Believe in the Lord Jesus Christ, and thou shalt be saved,"—commandments not addressed, as some say they are, to sensible sinners, but to insensible sinners, to stupid sinners, to sinners who cannot, so far as moral ability is concerned, obey the command at all. Such are bidden so to do by him, who in this case bade the man do what he, naturally in and of himself, was quite incapable of doing; because you see if he could stretch out his hand himself, there was no miracle wanted, for the man's hand was not withered at all. But it is clear that he could not move his hand, and yet the Saviour addressed him as if he could do it; in which I see a symbol of the gospel way of speaking to the sinner; for the gospel cries to him in all his misery and incapacity, "To thee, even to thee, is the word of this salvation sent." This very incapacity and inability of thine is but the space in which the divine power may be displayed, and because thou art thus incapable, and because thou art thus unable, therefore to thee does the gospel come, that the excellency of the power may be seen to dwell in the gospel, and in the Saviour himself, and not at all in the person who is saved.

The command, then, which brought healing with it, was addressed to one who was utterly incapable.

But, mark you, it came to *one who was perfectly willing*, for this man was quite prepared to do whatever Jesus bade him do. If you had questioned him you would have found no desire to retain that withered hand—no wish that his fingers should remain lifeless and useless. If you had said to him, " Poor man, would you like to have your hand restored ?" tears would have been in his eyes, and he would have replied, " Ay, that I would, that I might earn bread for my dear children ; that I might not have to go about begging, and have to depend upon the help of others, or only earn a hard crust with this left hand of mine. I wish above all things that I could have my hand restored !" But the worst of many unconverted people is that they do not want to be healed—do not want to be restored. As soon as a man truly longs for salvation, then has salvation already come to him; but the most of you do not wish to be saved. " Oh," say you, " we truly wish to be saved." I do not think so, for what do you mean by being saved ? Do you mean being saved from going down to hell ? Everybody, of course, wishes that. Did you ever meet a thief that would not like to be saved from going to prison or being locked up by the policeman ? But when we talk about salvation, we mean being saved from the habit of wrong-doing; being saved from the power of evil, the love of sin, the practice of folly, and the very power to find pleasure in transgression. Do you wish to be saved from pleasurable and gainful sins ? Find me the drunkard who sincerely prays to be delivered from drunkenness. Bring me an unchaste man who pines to be pure. Find me one who is an habitual liar and yet longs to speak the truth. Bring me one who has been selfish and who in his very heart hates himself for it, and longs to be full of love and to be made Christlike. Why, half the battle is won in such cases. The initial step is taken. The parallel holds good in the spiritual world. The character I have in my mind's eye is the case of a soul desiring to be what it cannot be, and to do what it cannot do, and yet desiring it. I mean the man who cries in agony, "To will is present with me, but how to perform that which is good I find not." " I would, but cannot, repent. My heart feels like a stone. I would love Christ, but, alas, I feel that I am fettered to the world. I would be holy, but, alas, sin comes violently upon me, and carries me away." It is to such people that Jesus Christ gospel comes with the force of a command. Wilt thou be made whole, my friend? Then thou mayest be. Dost thou desire to be saved from sin? Thou mayest be. Dost thou wish to be emancipated from the bondage of corruption? Thou mayest be. And this is the way in which thou mayest be saved,—" Believe in the Lord Jesus Christ, and thou shalt be saved" : his name is called Jesus, for he shall save his people from their sins. He has come on purpose to do this to real sinners, and not to mere pretenders, for it is clear that he cannot save men from sins if they have none. He cannot heal withered hands if there are no withered hands to be healed. He comes to you that want him, to you that are guilty, to you whose hands are withered. Even to you is this glorious word of the good news proclaimed; God grant you grace to hear it believingly and to feel its power!

II. Secondly, I want to speak a little upon THE PERSON WHO GAVE THE COMMAND. It was *Jesus* who gave it. *He* said, " Stretch forth thine hand."

Did our Lord speak this in ignorance, supposing that the man could do so? By no means, for in him is abundant knowledge. He had just read the hearts of the Pharisees, and you may be sure that he who could read those subtle spirits could certainly see the outward condition of this patient. He knew that the man's hand was withered, and yet he said, " Stretch forth thine hand." When I read in Scripture the command, " Believe in the Lord Jesus Christ," I am sure that Jesus Christ knows what he is saying. " Go ye," said he, " into all the world, and preach the gospel to every creature." Yes, to every creature. Suppose that some of his disciples had been very orthodox, and had come back and said, " Lord, was there not a mistake about the persons? Why preach to every creature? Are not some of them dead in sin? We would rather preach to character." I have heard some of Christ's professed servants say that to bid dead sinners live is of no more use than to shake a handkerchief over the graves in which the dead are buried ; and my reply to them has been, " You are quite right. Do not do it, for it is evident you are not called to it. Go home and go to bed. The Lord never sent you to do anything of the kind, for you own you have no faith in it." But if my Master sent *me* as the herald of resurrection, and bade me shake a handkerchief over the graves of the dead, I would do it, and I should expect that this poor handkerchief, if *he* commanded it to be shaken, would raise the dead, for Jesus Christ knows what he is doing when he sends his servants. If he does not send us, it is a fool's errand indeed to go and say, " Ye dead men, live "; but his commission makes all the difference. We are to say to the dead, " Awake, and Christ shall give you life." What, wake first, and then get life afterwards? I shall not try to explain it, but that is the order of the Scripture : " Awake, thou that sleepest, and arise from the dead, and Christ shall give thee life." If my Master puts it so, I am quite satisfied to quote his words. I cannot explain it, but I delight to take him in his own way, and blindly follow his every step, and believe his every word. If he bids me say, " Arise from the dead," I will gladly do it now. In the name of Jesus, ye dead ones, live. Break, ye hard hearts. Dissolve, ye hearts of steel. Believe, ye unbelievers. Lay hold on Christ, ye ungodly ones. If he speak by his ministers, that word shall be with power; if he speak not by us, it is little matter how we speak. Well may the judicious brother say that there would be no use in *his* bidding the dead arise, for he confesses that his Master is not with him. Let him, therefore, go home till his Master is with him. If his Master were with him, then would he speak his Master's word, and he would not be afraid of being called foolish. It is the Lord Jesus Christ who says to this man with the withered hand, "Stretch forth thine hand."

To me it is a sweet thought that he is able to give power to do what he gives the command to do. Dear soul, when you are bidden to believe, and you stand with tears in your eyes and say, " Sir, I cannot understand, and I cannot believe," dost thou not know that he who bids thee believe can give thee power to believe ? When *he* speaks through his servants, or through his word, or directly by his Spirit upon your conscience, he who bids thee do this is no mere man, but the Son of God, and thou must say to him, " Good Lord, I beseech thee give me now the faith which thou dost ask of me. Give me the repentance thou dost command ; " and he will hear thy prayer, and faith shall spring up within thee.

Did you never notice, dear souls, Christ's way of doing his work ? His way is generally this,—first, to give the command, then to help the heart to turn the command into a prayer, and then to answer that prayer by a promise. Take these specimens. The Lord says, " Make you a new heart." That is clearly a command. But by-and-by you find the psalmist David, in the fifty-first psalm, saying, " Create in me a clean heart, O God." And then, if you turn to Ezekiel, you get the promise, " A new heart also will I give you." First, he commands you ; next he sets you praying for the blessing ; and then he gives it to you.

Take another ; the command is, " Turn ye, turn ye, why will ye die, O house of Israel ? " Then comes the prayer, " Turn thou me, and I shall be turned " ; and then follows the blessed turning of which the apostle Paul speaks when he says that God has sent his Son to bless us by turning every one of us from his iniquity.

Take another case, and let it refer to purging. We find the Lord commanding us to " purge out the old leaven " ; and straightway there comes the prayer, " Purge me with hyssop, and I shall be clean," and then on the heels of it comes the promise, " I will purely purge away thy dross." Or, take another kind of precept, of a sweeter sort, belonging to the Christian. You are continually told to sing : " Sing praises to God, sing praises : sing praises unto our King, sing praises." In another place we meet with the prayer, " Open thou my lips, and my mouth shall shew forth thy praise;" and in a third Scripture we have the divine promise, "This people have I formed for myself ; they shall shew forth my praise." See, then, the Master's way of going to work—he commands you to believe, or repent ; he then sets you a-praying that you may be enabled to do it, and then he gives you grace to do it, so that the blessing may really come to your soul ; for everywhere gospel commands are uttered by Christ himself to men's hearts, and they, receiving them, find the ability coming with the command.

" But he is not here," says one, " he is not here." Verily I say unto you in his name, he is here. His word is, " Lo, I am with you alway, even to the end of the world": till this dispensation shall be ended Christ will be where the gospel is preached. Where his message is honestly and truthfully delivered with the Spirit of God, there Jesus Christ himself is virtually present, speaking through the lips of his servants. Therefore, dear soul with the withered hand, to-night Jesus himself says to thee, "Stretch forth thine hand." He is present to heal, and his method is to command. He now commands. O gracious Spirit, be present that men may obey.

III. It is time for a few words upon another point, and that is upon THE COMMAND ITSELF. The command itself was, "Stretch forth thine hand." I notice about that command that it goes to the very essence of the matter. It is not, "Rub your right hand with your left"; it is not, "Show your hand to the priest, and let him perform a ceremony upon it"; it is not, "Wash your hand"; but it is, "Stretch it forth." That was the very thing he could not do, and thus the command went to the very root of the mischief. As soon as the hand was stretched out it was healed; and the command went directly to the desired mark.

Now, my Lord and Master does not say to any of you sinners to-night, "Go home and pray." I hope you will pray, but that is not the great gospel command. The gospel is, "Believe in the Lord Jesus Christ, and thou shalt be saved." Paul stood at the dead of night, with the trembling jailer, who hardly understood his own question, when he cried, "Sirs, what must I do to be saved?" and Paul according to the practice of some should have said, "We must have a little prayer," or, "You must go home and read the Bible, and I must further instruct you until you are in a better state." He did nothing of the sort, but there and then Paul said, "Believe in the Lord Jesus Christ, and thou shalt be saved." There is no gospel preached unless you come to this; for salvation comes by faith, and by nothing short of it. That is just the difficult point, you tell me. Yes, and at the difficult point this command strikes and says, "Stretch forth thine hand"; or in the case of the sinner, "Believe in the Lord Jesus Christ." For, remember, all that any of you ever do in the matter of eternal life, which has not faith in it, can be nothing after all but the effort of your carnal nature, and that is death. What can come of the movements of death but a still deeper death? Death can never produce life. Prayer without faith! What sort of prayer is it? It is the prayer of a man who does not believe God. Shall a man expect to receive anything of the Lord if he does not believe that God is, and that he is the rewarder of them that diligently seek him? "Oh, but I must repent before I believe," says one. What kind of repentance is that which does not trust God—does not believe in God? An unbelieving repentance—is it not a selfish expression of regret because of punishment incurred? Faith must be mixed with every prayer and every act of repentance, or they cannot be acceptable; and hence we must go right straight to this point, and demand faith, saying: "Believe and live;" "Stretch forth thine hand."

That stretching forth of the hand was entirely *an act of faith.* It was not an act of sense. As a matter of sense and nature the man was powerless for it. He only did it because his faith brought the ability. I say it was a pure act of faith, that stretching out of the hand. "I do not understand as yet," says one, "how a man can do what he cannot do?" But you will understand a great many other wonderful things when the Lord teaches you; for the Christian life is a series of paradoxes; and for my own part I doubt an experience unless there is something paradoxical about it. At any rate I am sure that it is so—that I who can do nothing of myself can do everything through Christ which strengtheneth me. The man who is seeking Christ can do nothing, and yet, if he believeth on Christ, he can do everything, and his withered hand is stretched out.

But, in addition to its being an act of faith, it seems to me it was *an act of decision.* There sit the haughty, frowning Pharisees. Your imagination can easily picture those fine-looking gentlemen, with fringes to their garments, and phylacteries across their foreheads. There, too, are the scribes all wrapped up in their formal array—very grave and knowing men. Persons were almost afraid to look at them, they were so holy, and so contemptuous. See, there they sit, like judges of assize, to try the Saviour. Now, Christ does, as it were, single out this poor man with a withered hand to be his witness; and by his command he practically asks him which he will do—will he obey the Pharisees or himself? It is wrong to heal on the Sabbath day, say the Pharisees. What say you with the withered hand over yonder? If you agree with the Pharisees, of course you will decline to be healed on the Sabbath day, and you won't stretch out your hand; but if you agree with Jesus, you will be glad to be healed, Sabbath or no Sabbath. Ah, I see, you will stretch out your hand and break away from the tyrants who would keep you withered. The man did as good as vote for Christ when he stretched forth his hand. Many a soul has found peace when at last he has held up his hand and said, "Sink or swim, lost or saved; Christ for me, Christ for me! If I perish I will cling to his cross-foot, and to him alone will I look; for I am on his side, whether he will have compassion upon me or not." When that act of decision is performed, then comes the healing. If you hold up your hand for Christ, he will make it a good hand though now it is all paralyzed and drooping, like a dead thing. Unworthy as you are, he has the power, as you hold up your hand for him, to put life into it, and to give you the blessing your heart desires.

I think I hear somebody say, "Oh, sir, you would not be praising me too much if you were to say that I do wish to be saved, and saved in Christ's own way; I would give my very eyes to love him." Ah, you need not lose your eyes: give him your trust; give him your soul's eyes. Look to him and live. "Oh, that I could be saved," says one; "How I long for it." May the Holy Ghost lead you to resolve in your own soul that you will not be saved by anybody but by Christ. O that you would determine—

> "He that suffer'd in my stead,
> Shall my Physician be;
> I will not be comforted
> Till Jesus comforts me."

When that is done, I do not doubt that, through faith in the physician, you will be quickened by divine power, and you will find healing at once.

IV. So I will just lead you on, in the fourth place, to notice THIS MAN'S OBEDIENCE. We are told that he stretched forth his hand. Christ said, "Stretch forth thine hand": Mark says, "And he did so." That is to say, he stretched forth his hand. Now, observe that *this man did not do something else in preference to what Jesus commanded*, though many awakened sinners are foolish enough to try experiments. Christ said, "Stretch forth thine hand"; *and he did so.* If, instead of that, the man had walked across the synagogue and brought himself up to Christ, the Master would have said, "I bade thee do no such thing. I bade thee stretch forth thy hand." Suppose he had then with his left hand begun to grasp the roll of the law as it stood in the synagogue, and had kissed it out of reverence, would that have been of any use? The Master would only have said, "I bade thee stretch forth thy hand." Alas, there are many, many souls that say, "We are bidden to trust in Jesus, but instead of that we will attend the means of grace regularly." Do that by all means, but not as a substitute for faith, or it will become a vain confidence. The command is, "Believe and live"; attend to that, whatever else you do. "Well, I shall take to reading good books; perhaps I shall get good that way." Read the good books by all means, but that is not the gospel: the gospel is, "Believe in the Lord Jesus Christ and thou shalt be saved." Suppose a physician has a patient under his care, and he says to him, "You are to take a bath in the morning; it will be of very great service to your disease." But the man takes a cup of tea in the morning instead of the bath, and he says, "That will do as well, I have no doubt." What does his physician say when he enquires—"Did you follow my rule?" "No, I did not." "Then you do not expect, of course, that there will be any good result, for you have disobeyed me." So we, practically, say to Jesus Christ, when we are under searching of soul, "Lord, thou badest me trust thee, but I would sooner do something else. Lord, I want to have horrible convictions; I want to be shaken over hell's mouth; I want to be alarmed and distressed." Yes, you want anything but what Christ prescribes for you, which is that you should simply trust him. Whether you feel or do not feel, you should just come and cast yourself on him, that *he* may save you, and he alone. "But you do not mean to say that you speak against praying, and reading good books, and so on?" Not one single word do I speak against any of those things, any more than, if I were the physician I quoted, I should speak against the man's drinking a cup of tea. Let him drink his tea; but not if he drinks it instead of taking the bath which I prescribe for him. So let the man pray: the more the better. Let the man search the Scriptures; but, remember, that if these things are put in the place of simple faith in Christ, the soul will be ruined. Let me give you a text: did you ever hear it quoted properly? "Ye search the Scriptures, for in them ye think ye have eternal life; but ye will not come unto me that ye might have life." That is where the life is—in Christ; not even in searching Scripture, good as the searching of Scripture is. If we put even golden idols into the place of Christ, such idols are as much to be broken as if they were idols of mud or idols of dung. It matters not how good an action is, if it is not what Christ commands, you will not be saved by it. "Stretch forth thine hand," says he; that was the way by which the healing was to come: the man did nothing else, and he received a gracious reward.

Notice, that *he did not raise any questions.* Now this man had a fair opportunity of raising questions. I think he might very fairly have stood up in his place and said, "This is inconsistent, good Master. Thou sayest to me, 'Stretch forth thine hand.' Now, thou knowest that if I can stretch forth my hand there ails me nothing, and therefore there is no room for thy miracle. And if I cannot stretch forth my hand, how canst thou tell me so to do?" Have you not heard some of our friends, who like to make jests of holy things, and to scoff at our doctrines of grace, declare that we teach, "You can and you can't; you shall and you shan't"? Their description is right enough, though meant to ridicule us. We do not object to their putting it thus if so it pleases them. We teach paradoxes and contradictions to the eye, if you only consider the letter; but if you get down into the innermost spirit, it is within these contradictions that the eternal truth is found. We know that the man is dead in trespasses and sins—steeped in a spiritual and moral torpor, out of which he cannot raise himself; yet do we by the Master's own command say, "Awake, thou that sleepest, and arise from the dead, and Christ shall give thee life;" or, in other words, we say to the withered hand, "Be thou stretched out," and it is done. The blessed result justifies that very teaching which in itself seems so worthy of sarcastic remark.

Notice further that what the man did was, that *he was told to stretch out his hand, and he did stretch out his hand.* If you had asked him, "Did *you* stretch out your hand?" perhaps he would have said, "Of course I did. Nobody else did." "Wait a minute, my good man. Did you *of yourself* stretch out your hand?" "Oh, no," he would say, "because I have tried many times before and I could not, but this time I did do it." "Then how was it that you were able to do it?" "Jesus told me to do it, and I was willing, and it was done." I do not expect that he could have explained the rationale of it, and perhaps we cannot either. It must, indeed, have been a very beautiful sight to see that poor, withered, limp, wilted hand, first hanging down, and then stretched out before all the people in the middle of the synagogue. Do you not see the blood begin to flow, the nerves gaining power, and the hand opening like a reviving flower? Oh, the delight of his sparkling eyes as at first he could only fix them upon the little finger and the thumb to see if they were really all alive! Then he turned, looked at that blessed One who had healed him, and seemed anxious to fall down at his feet and give him all the praise! Even so, we cannot explain conversion and regeneration and the new birth; and all that; but we do know this, that Jesus Christ says, "Believe," and we believe. By our own power? No. But as we will to believe (and he gives us that will) there comes a power to do according to his good pleasure.

I look around me, wondering where is the man with the withered hand to-night, or where is the woman with the withered hand. To such I would say in my Master's name, "Stretch out that hand of thine." It is an auspicious moment. A great thing shall be done unto thee. Believe thou now. Thou hast said aforetime, "I never can believe." Now trust Jesus. Sink or swim, trust him.

> "Venture on him, venture wholly;
> Let no other trust intrude,
> None but Jesus
> Can do helpless sinners good."

Our Lord Jesus never casts away a sinner who trusts in him. Oh I would almost put it like this,—If you do not feel that you can come, or ought to come, to Christ, being so unworthy, steal in ; steal into his house of mercy, just as you have known a hungry dog steal in where there has been something to eat. The butcher very likely would deal him a kick if he saw him after a bone ; but if he once gets it he may as well make off with it, and keep it to himself. There is this blessed thing about my Master—if you can get a crumb from under his table he will not take it from you, for he never casts out those that come. However they come, he neither turns them away nor takes back the blessing. He never says, "Come here, you sir, you have no right to hope in my grace." Remember the woman in the press that dared not come to Christ before his face, but who came behind him, and touched the hem of his garment. She stole the cure from him, as it were, will he, nil he, and what did he say ? "Come here, my woman, come here, what have you been at ? What right had you to touch my garment, and to steal a cure like this ? A curse shall come upon thee." Did he speak thus in indignation ? Not at all : not at all ! He bade her come, and she told him all the truth, and he said, "Daughter, be of good cheer. Thy faith hath made thee whole." Get at him, soul ! Behind or before, push for a touch of him ! Make a dash at him. If there be a crowd of devils between you and Christ, plough your way through them by resolute faith. Though you be the most unworthy wretch that ever trusted him, trust him now, that it may be told in heaven that there is a bigger sinner saved to-day than ever was saved before. Such a salvation will make Christ more glorious than he ever was ; and if yours is a worse case than he ever touched with his healing hand to this day, well then, when he has touched and healed you, as he will, there will be more praise to him in heaven than he ever had before. O soul, I would I could persuade thee to draw nigh to him, but my Master can do it. May he draw thee by his great grace !

V. The last thing to consider is THE RESULT OF THIS STRETCHING OUT OF THE MAN'S HAND IN OBEDIENCE TO THE COMMAND. He was healed.

I have already tried to set before you the fact that the healing was *manifest;* it was also *immediate.* The man had not to stand there a long time, but his hand was straightway healed : and yet the cure was *perfect,* for his hand was whole like unto the other, just as useful as his left hand had been, with all the extra dexterity which naturally belongs to the right. It was perfectly healed, though healed in a moment. You may depend upon it, that it was *permanently* healed ; for, though I have heard it said that saved souls fall from grace and perish, I never believed it, for I have never read of any of the cases which our Lord cured that they became bad again. I never heard of a withered hand that was healed and was paralyzed a second time. Nor will it ever be. My Master's cures last for ever. I remember seeing in the shop windows some years ago, that there was to be had within a "momentary cure" for the toothache. I noticed after a few months that the proprietor of that valuable medicine, whatever it was, had discovered that nobody wanted a *momentary* cure, and so the word "momentary" was changed for the word "*instantaneous,*" which was a great improvement. I am afraid that some people's salvation is a momentary salvation. They get a sort of grace, and they lose it again. They get peace, and by-and-by it is gone. What is wanted is permanence, and there is always permanence in the work of Christ. "The gifts and calling of God are without repentance," and his healing is never revoked. O soul, dost thou see, then, what is to be had at this moment of Jesus? Healing for life; deliverance from the withering power of sin through life and through eternity. This is to be had by cheerful obedience to the matchless command: "Stretch forth thine hand," or, in other words, "Trust, trust, trust." Only this week I was talking with one who said he could not trust Christ, and I said, "But, my dear friend, we cannot have that. Could you trust *me*?" Yes, he could trust me. "Why can you trust me and not trust the Lord Jesus? I will put it the other way. If you said to me I cannot trust you, what would that imply?" "Why," said he, "it would mean, of course, that you were a very bad fellow, if I could not trust you." "Ah," I said, "that is exactly what you insinuate when you say, I cannot trust Jesus; for he that believeth not hath made him a liar. Do you mean to say that God is a liar?" The person to whom I spoke drew back with horror from that consequence, and said "No, sir, I am sure that God is true." Very well, then, you can certainly trust one who is true. There can be no difficulty in that; to trust and rest upon one whom you cannot doubt must follow as a matter of course upon your good opinion of him. Your belief that he is true is a sort of faith. Throw yourself upon him now. Just as I lean upon this rail with all my weight, lean like that upon the mercy of God in Christ Jesus. That is faith. If God's mercy in Christ cannot save thee, be lost. Make it thy sole hope and confidence. Hang on thy God in Christ Jesus as the vessel hangs upon the nail. As a man casts his whole weight upon his bed, so throw thyself unreservedly upon the divine love which was seen in Jesus, and is seen there still. If thou doest this thou shalt be saved. And I do not mean merely that you shall be saved from hell; for the power of faith, working in you by God the Holy Spirit, shall save you from loving sin any more: being forgiven, you will henceforth love him who forgives you, and you will receive a new principle of action which shall be strong enough to break the bands of your old habits, and you shall rise into a pure and holy life. If the Son shall make you free, you shall be free indeed; and free you shall be at once if now you trust him. The Lord grant his blessing, for Christ's sake. Amen.

The Friends of Jesus

"Ye are my friends, if ye do whatsoever I command you."—John xv. 14.

OUR Lord Jesus Christ is beyond all comparison the best of friends: a friend in need, a friend indeed. "Friend!" said Socrates, "there is no friend!" but Socrates did not know our Lord Jesus, or he would have added, "except the Saviour." In the heart of our Lord Jesus there burns such friendship towards us that all other forms of it are as dim candles to the sun. "Greater love hath no man than this, that he lay down his life for his friend." An ordinary man has gone as far as ever he can when he has died for his friend; and yet he would have died anyhow, so that in dying for his friend he does but pay, somewhat beforehand, a debt which must inevitably have been discharged a little further on. With Christ there was no necessity to die at all, and this, therefore, places his love and his friendship alone by itself. He died who needed not to die, and died in agony when he might have lived in glory: never did man give such proof of friendship as this.

Let the friendship of our Lord to us stand as the model of our friendship to him. It cannot be so in all respects, because our situations and conditions are different: his must always be the love of the greater to the less, the love of the benefactor to one in need, the love of the Redeemer to those who are bought with a price; but, setting those points aside, the whole tone and spirit of our Lord's friendship are such that the more closely we can imitate it the better. Such friendship as his should be reflected in a friendship most hearty and self-sacrificing on our part.

Our Lord does not, I think, in this text speak to us about his being our friend, but about our being his friends. He is "the friend of sinners"; but sinners are not his friends till their hearts are changed. "Ye are my friends, if ye do whatsoever I command you"; we are not his friends till then. His love to us is entirely of himself, but friendship needs something from us. Friendship cannot be all on one side: one-sided friendship is more fitly called mercy, grace, or benevolence; friendship in its full sense is mutual. You may do all you will for a man and be perfectly benevolent, and yet he may make you no return; but friendship can only exist where there is a response. Hence, we have not before us the question as to whether Christ loves us or not, as to whether Christ has pity on us or not; for in another part of Scripture we read of "his great love wherewith he loved us even when we were dead in trespasses and sins." He befriended us when we were enemies, but that is not our subject just now: the question is about our being friends to him, and such we must be made if, indeed, there is to be any intimacy of mutual friendship. Friendship cannot be, as I have said before, all on one side; it is like a pair of scales, there must be something to balance on the other side; there must be a return of kindly feeling from the person loved. Jesus tells us here that if we are to be his friends we must do whatsoever he commands us, and that out of love to him.

Beloved, it is the highest honour in the world to be called the friend of Christ. There is no title surely that excels in dignity that which was worn by Abraham, who was called "The friend of God." Lord Brooke was so delighted with the friendship of Sir Philip Sydney that he ordered to be engraved upon his tomb nothing but this, "Here lies the friend of Sir Philip Sydney." There is beauty in such a feeling, but yet it is a small matter compared with being able to say, "Here lives a friend of Christ." O wondrous condescension that he should call me "friend." If I am indeed a true believer, not only is he *my* friend, without which I could have no hope here or hereafter, but he hath in the aboundings of his grace been pleased to regard me as *his* friend, and write me down in the honoured list of intimates who are permitted to speak familiarly with him, as those do between whom there are no secrets, for their hearts are told out to him whilst he hides nothing from them, but saith, "If it were not so I would have told you." Beloved, in what a light this sets obedience to Christ's commandments. I cannot help at this early moment in the sermon noticing how the doctrine of our text transfigures obedience, and makes it the joy and glory of life. How precious it is, for it is a better seal to friendship than the possession of the largest gifts and influence. Christ does not say, "Ye are my friends, if ye rise to a position of respectability among men, or honour in the church." No, however poor you may be, and those to whom he spake these words were very poor, he says, "Ye are my friends, if ye do whatsoever I command you." Obedience is better than wealth and better than rank. Jesus values his friends, not by what they have, or what they wear, but by what they *do*. The whole eleven apostles we may put down as having remarkable qualifications for their life-work; yet their Lord does not say, "Ye are my friends, because I have endowed you with abilities for the apostleship." Even to these leaders of his sacramental host Jesus says plainly, "Ye are my friends, if ye do whatsoever I command you." That is the point by which your friendship shall be tested: "If ye are obedient ye are my friends." He says neither less nor more to any of us who this day aspire to the high dignity of being contained within the circle of his personal friendship. You must, my brethren, yield obedience to your Master and Lord, and be eager to do it, or you are not his bosom friends. This is the one essential, which grace alone can give us. Do we rebel against the request? Far from it; our joy and delight lie in bearing our Beloved's easy yoke.

I. Let us come to the subject more closely, and notice first, that OUR LORD HIMSELF TELLS US WHAT OBEDIENCE HE REQUESTS from those who call themselves his friends. True friends are eager to know what they can do to please the objects of their love; let us gladly hearken to what our adorable Lord now speaks to the select circle of his chosen. He asks of one and all obedience. None of us are exempted from doing his commandments. However lofty or however lowly our condition, we must obey; if our talent be but one, we must obey, and if we have ten, still we must obey. There can be no friendship with Christ unless we are willing, each one, to yield him hearty, loyal service. Let it go round, then, to all of you upon whom the name of Jesus Christ is named: if enrolled among the friends of Jesus you must be careful about your own personal obedience to his blessed will. Forget not that even to the queen, standing on his right in gold of Ophir, the word is given, "He is thy Lord, and worship thou him."

It must be *active obedience*, notice that. "Ye are my friends, if ye *do* whatsoever I command you." Some think it is quite sufficient if they avoid what he forbids. Abstinence from evil is a great part of righteousness, but it is not enough for friendship. If a man can say, "I am not a drunkard, I am not dishonest, I am not unchaste, I am not a violator of the Sabbath, I am not a liar;" so far so good, but such righteousness does not exceed that of the scribes and pharisees, and they cannot enter the kingdom. It is well if you do not wilfully transgress, but if you are to be Christ's friends there must be far more than this. It would be a poor friendship which only said, "I am your friend, and to prove it, I don't insult you, I don't rob you, I don't speak evil of you." Surely there must be more positive evidence to certify friendship. The Lord Jesus Christ lays great stress upon positive duties: it is, "*if ye do* whatsoever I command you." At the last day he will say, "I was an hungered, and ye gave me meat: I was thirsty, and ye gave me drink." In that memorable twenty-fifth of Matthew nothing is said about negative virtues; but positive actions are cited and dwelt upon in detail. You know it is an old English saying, "He is my friend who grinds at my mill." That is to say, friendship shows itself in doing helpful acts, which prove sincerity. Fine words are mere wind, and go for nothing if not backed up with substantial deeds of kindness. Friendship cannot live on windy talk, it needs the bread of matter of fact. The inspired word says, "Show me a proof of your love; show it by doing whatsoever I command you."

We are clear, from the wording of the text, that the obedience Christ expects from us is *continuous*. He does not say, "If you sometimes do what I command you—if you do it on Sundays, for instance—if you do what I command you in your place of worship, that will suffice; but no, we are to abide in him and keep his statutes even unto the end. I am not now preaching works as the way of salvation but as the evidences of fellowship, which is quite another thing. We must seek in every place, at all times, and under all circumstances, to do as Jesus bids us, out of a cheerful spirit of reverence to him. Such tender, loving subjection as a godly wife gives to her husband must be gladly yielded by us throughout life if we are his friends.

This obedience must also be *universal*. " Ye are my friends, if ye do *whatsoever* I command you." No sooner is anything discovered to be the subject of a command than the man who is a true friend of Christ says, " I will do it," and he does it. He does not pick and choose which precept he will keep and which he will neglect, for this is self-will and not obedience. I have known some professors err greatly in this matter. They have been very strict over one point, and they have blamed everybody who did not come up to their strictness, talking as if that one duty fulfilled the whole law. Straining at gnats has been a very leading business with many ; they have bought a choice assortment of strainers of the very finest net to get out all the gnats from their cup, but at the same time, on another day they have opened their mouths and swallowed a camel without a qualm. This will not do : the test is, " If ye do *whatsoever* I command you." I do not mean that little things are unimportant : far from it. If there be a gnat that Christ bids you strain at, strain it out with great diligence ; do not let a midge escape you if he bids you remove it. The smallest command of Christ may often be the most important ; and I will tell you why. Some things are great, evidently great, and for many reasons even a hypocritical professor will attend to them, but the test may lie in the minor points, which hypocrites do not take the trouble to notice, since no human tongue would praise them for so doing. Here is the proof of your love. Will you do the smaller thing for Jesus as well as the more weighty matter ? Too many say, " I do not see any use in it, I can be saved without it ; there are a great many different opinions on the point," and so on. All this cometh of evil, and is not consistent with the spirit of friendship with Christ, for love pleases even in trifles. Is it Christ's will ? Is it plainly a precept of his word? Then it is not yours to reason why, nor to raise any question. The reality of your subjection to your Lord and Master may hinge upon those seemingly insignificant points. A domestic servant might place the breakfast on the table, and feel that she had done her duty, but if her mistress told her to place the salt at the corner, and she did not, she would be asked the cause of her neglect. Suppose she replied to her mistress, " I did not think it needful ; I placed the breakfast before you, but a little salt was too trifling a matter for me to troubled about." Her mistress might answer, " But I told you to be sure and put out the salt-cellar. Mind you do so to-morrow." Next morning there is no salt, and the maid says she did not see the use of setting it on the table. Her mistress is displeased, and tells her that her wish must be carried out. Will she not be a very foolish and vexatious girl if she refuses to do so, because she does not see the use of it ? I think it is likely that the young woman would have to find another situation before long, for such conduct is very annoying. So it is with those professors who say, " I have attended to the main things, and what I neglect is quite a minor matter." Such are not even good servants ; friends they never can be. I beseech you, dear brethren, labour after universal obedience. " Whatsoever he saith to you, do it." Only by an earnest endeavour to carry out the whole of his will can you live in happy fellowship with him, and be indeed his friends.

Note well, that this obedience is to be rendered as *to Christ himself.*

Put the emphasis on the little word *I:* "Ye are my friends, if ye do whatsoever *I* command you." We are to do these things because Jesus commands them. Does not the royal person of our Lord cast a very strong light upon the necessity of obedience? When we refuse to obey we refuse to do what the Lord himself commands. When the Lord Jesus Christ, the Son of God and our Redeemer, is denied obedience it is treason. How can rebels against the King be his Majesty's friends? The precepts of Scripture are not the commandments of man nor the ordinances of angels, but the laws of Christ, and how dare we despise them? We are to act rightly because Jesus commands us, and we love to do his pleasure; there can be no friendship without this. Oh for grace to serve the Lord with gladness.

To close this first point, it appears that our Lord would have us obey him *out of a friendly spirit.* Obedience to Christ as if we were forced to do it under pains and penalties would be of no worth as a proof of friendship; every one can see that. He speaks not of slaves, but of friends; he would not have us perform duties from fear of punishment or love of reward; that which he can accept of his friends must be the fruit of love. His will must be our law because his person is our delight. Some professors need to be whipped to their duties; they must hear stirring sermons, and attend exciting meetings, and live under pressure; but those who are Christ's friends need no spur but love. "The love of Christ constraineth us." True hearts do what Jesus bids them without flogging and dogging, urging and forcing. Constrained virtue is spoiled in the making, as many a piece of earthenware is cracked in the baking. The wine of our obedience must flow freely from the ripe cluster of the soul's love, or it will not be fit for the royal cup. When duty becomes delight and precepts are as sweet as promises, then are we Christ's friends, and not till then.

II. Having thus set forth what kind of obedience Christ requests, I now notice, in the second place, that our Lord leads us to gather from this sentence that THOSE WHO DO NOT OBEY HIM ARE NO FRIENDS OF HIS. He may yet look upon them and be their friend by changing their hearts and forgiving their sins; but as yet they are no friends of his, for a man who does not obey Christ *does not give the Saviour his proper place,* and this is an unfriendly deed. If I have a friend I am very careful that, if he has honour anywhere, he shall certainly have due respect from me. If he be my superior, I am anxious that he should not think me intrusive, or imagine that I would take undue advantage of his kindness. He will be higher in my esteem than in the regard of anyone else. He who is truly Christ's friend delights to honour him as a great king, but he who will not yield him his sovereign rights is a traitor and not a friend. Our Lord is the head over all things to his church, and this involves the joyful submission of the members: disobedience denies to Christ the dignity of that holy Headship which is his prerogative over all the members of his mystical body, and this is not the part of a true friend. How can you be his friend if you will not admit his rule? It is vain to boast that you trust his cross if you do not reverence his crown.

He who does not do his commandments cannot be Christ's friend, because *he is not of one mind with Christ:* that is evident. Can two walk together except they be agreed? True friendship exists not between those who differ upon first principles, and there can be no points of agreement between Jesus Christ and the man who will not obey him; for he in fact says, "Lord Jesus, thy pure and holy will is obnoxious to me; thy sweet and gracious commands are a weariness to me. What friendship can be here? They are not of one mind: Christ is for holiness, this man is for sin; Christ is for spiritual-mindedness, this man is carnal-minded; Christ is for love, this man is for self; Christ is for glorifying the Father, this man is for honouring himself: how can there be any friendship when they are diametrically opposed in design, object, and spirit? It is not possible.

He who obeys not Christ cannot be Christ's friend, though he may profess to be. *He may be a very high and loud professor, and for that reason he may be all the more an enemy of the cross:* for when men see this man walking according to his own lusts they cry out, "Thou also wast with Jesus of Nazareth," and they attribute all his faults to his religion, and straightway begin to blaspheme the name of Christ. Through the inconsistent conduct of our Lord's professed friends his cause is more hindered than by anything else. Suppose you and I had some very intimate associate who was found drunk in the street, or committing burglary or theft, should we not feel disgraced by his conduct? When he was brought before the magistrate would you like to have it said, "This person is the bosom friend of So-and-so"? Oh, you would cover your face and beg your neighbours never to mention it. For such a fellow to be known as your friend would compromise your name and character. We say this even weeping, that Jesus Christ's name is compromised, and his honour is tarnished among men by many who wear the name of Christian without having the spirit of Christ: such cannot be his dear companions. Alas, for the wounds which Jesus has received in the house of his friends. When Cæsar fell he was slain by the daggers of his friends! In trust he found treason. Those whose lives he had spared, spared not his life. Woe to those who under the garb of Christianity crucify the Lord afresh, and put him to an open shame. Nothing burns Christ's cheek like a Judas kiss, and he has had many such.

Those that obey him not cannot be owned by Jesus as his friends, for *that would dishonour him indeed.* Time was—I know not how it is now—when if any man wanted to be made a count, or to get an honourable title, he had only to pay so much at Rome into the Papal exchequer, and he could be made a noble at once. The titles thus purchased were neither honourable to those who gave nor to those who received them. Whatever his pretended vicar may do, our Lord himself sells no dignities. The title of "friends of Jesus" goes with a certain character, and cannot be otherwise obtained. Those are his friends who obey him :—" If ye love me, keep my commandments." He grants this patent of nobility to all believers who lovingly follow him, but on his list of friends he enters none beside. Do you not see that his honour requires this? Would you have our Lord stand up and say, "The drunkard is my friend"? Would you hear him say, "That fraudulent bankrupt is my intimate companion"? Would you have Jesus claim friendly companionship with the vicious and profane? A man is known by his company; what would be thought of Jesus if his intimate associates were men of loose morals and unrighteous principles? To go among them for their good is one thing, to make them his friends is another. Where there is no kinship, no likeness, no point of agreement, the fair flower of friendship cannot take root. We may, therefore, read the text negatively, " Ye are not my friends, if ye do not the things which I command you."

III. Our third observation is : THOSE WHO BEST OBEY CHRIST ARE ON THE BEST OF TERMS WITH HIM. "Ye are my friends," he seems to say, " and live near to me, enjoying practical personal friendship and daily intercourse with me, when you promptly obey." Some of you know by personal experience, brothers and sisters, that you cannot walk in holy converse with Christ unless you keep his commandments. There is no feeling of communion between our souls and Christ when we are conscious of having done wrong and yet are not sorry for it. If we know that we have erred, as we often do, and our hearts break because we have grieved our Beloved, and we go and tell him our grief, and confess our sin, we are still his friends, and he kisses away our tears, saying, " I know your weakness : I willingly blot out your offences. There is no breach of friendship between us ; I will manifest myself to you still." When we know that we are wrong, and feel no softening of heart about it, then we cannot pray, we cannot speak with the Beloved, and we cannot walk with him as his friends. Familiarity with Jesus ceases when we become familiar with known sin. If, again, knowing any act to be wrong we persevere in it, there cannot be any happy friendship between us and our Saviour. If conscience has told you, dear brother, that such and such a thing ought to be given up, and you continue in it, the next time you are on your knees you will feel yourself greatly hampered, and when you sit down before your open Bible and hope to have communion with Christ as you have formerly enjoyed it, you will find that he has withdrawn himself, and will not be found by you. Is there any wonder? If sin lieth at the door how can the Lord smile on us? Secret sin will poison communion at the fountain head. If there is a quarrel between you and Christ, and you are hugging to your bosom that which he abhors, how can you enjoy friendship? He tells you that sin is a viper that will kill you, but you reply, " It is a necklace of jewels," and, therefore, you put it about your neck. Do you wonder that because he loves you he is grieved at such mad behaviour? Oh, do not thus bring injury upon yourself. Do not thus pour contempt upon his wise commands.

Some Christians will never get into full fellowship with Christ because they neglect to study his word and search out what his will is. It ought to be a serious work with every Christian, especially in commencing his career, to find what is the will of his Lord on all subjects. Half the Christian people in the world are content to ask, " What is the rule of our church?" That is not the question : the point is, " What is the rule of Christ?" Some plead, " My father and mother before me did so." I sympathise in a measure with that feeling : filial reverence commands admiration ; but yet in spiritual things we are to call no man " father," but make the Lord Jesus our master and exemplar. God has not placed your conscience in your mother's keeping, nor has he committed to your father the right or the power to stand responsible for you: every man must bear his own burden and render his own account: search ye the Scriptures for yourselves each one of you, and follow no rule but that which is inspired. Take your light directly from the sun. Let holy Scripture be your unquestioned rule of faith and practice; and if there is any point about which you are uncertain, I charge you by your loyalty to Christ, if ye are his friends, try and find out what his will is; and when once you are sure upon that point never mind the human authorities or dignities that oppose his law. Let there be no question, no hesitation, no delay. If he commands you, carry out his will though the gates of hell thunder at you. You are not his friends, or, at any rate, you are not so his friends as to enjoy the friendship unless you resolutely seek to please him in all things. The intimacy between you and Christ will be disturbed by sin; you cannot lean your head upon his bosom and say, "Lord, I know thy will, but I do not mean to do it." Could you look up into that dear face—that visage once so marred, now lovelier than heaven itself—and say, "My Lord, I love thee, but I will not do thy will in every point"? By the very love he bears to you, he will chasten you for that rebellious spirit if you indulge it. It is a horrible evil; holy eyes will not endure it. He is a jealous lover, and will not tolerate sin, which is his rival.

"Ye are my friends, if ye do whatsoever I command you." Oh, beloved, see to this! Under all the crosses, and losses, and trials of life there is no comfort more desirable than the confidence that you have aimed at doing your Lord's will. If a man suffers for Christ's sake while steadily pursuing the course of holiness, he may rejoice in such suffering. Losses borne in the defence of the right and the true are gains. Jesus is never nearer his friends than when they bravely bear shame for his sake. If we get into trouble by our own folly we feel the smart at our very heart; but if we are wounded in our Lord's battles the scars are honourable. For his sake we may accept reproach, and bind it about us as a wreath of honour. Jesus delights to be the Companion of those who are cast out by kinsfolk and acquaintances for the truth's sake and for fidelity to his cross. They may call the faithful one fanatic, and enthusiast, and all such ill-sounding names; but over these there is no need to fret, for the honour of being Christ's friend infinitely outweighs the world's opinion. When we follow the Lamb whithersoever he goeth he is responsible for results; we are not.

> "Though dark be my way, since he is my guide,
> 'Tis mine to obey, 'tis his to provide."

The consequences which follow from our doing right belong to God. Abhor the theory that for the sake of a great good you may do a little wrong. I have heard men say, ay and Christian men too, "If I were strictly to follow my convictions I should have to leave a post of great usefulness, and therefore I remain where I am, and quiet my conscience as well as I can. I should lose opportunities of doing good, which I now possess, if I were to put in practice all I believe, and therefore I remain in a position which I could not justify on any other ground." Is this according to the mind of Jesus? Is this thy kindness to thy friend? How many bow in the house of Rimmon, and hope that the Lord will have mercy upon his servants in this thing. We shall see if it will be so. We may not do evil that good may come. If I knew that to do right would shake this whole island I should be bound to do it; God helping me, I would do it; and if I heard that a wrong act would apparently bless a whole nation, I have no right to do wrong on that account. No bribe of supposed usefulness should purchase our conscience. Right is right, and must always end in blessing; and wrong is wrong, and must always end in curse, though for a while it may wear the appearance of surpassing good. Did not the devil lead our first parents astray by the suggestion that great benefit would arise out of their transgression? "Your eyes shall be opened, and ye shall be as gods," said the arch-deceiver. Would it not be a grand thing for men to grow unto gods? "Certainly," says Eve; "I would not lose the opportunity. The race which is yet to be would blame me if I did. I would not have men remain inferior creatures through my neglect." For the sake of the promised good she ventured upon evil. Thousands of people sin because it seems so advantageous, so wise, so necessary, so sure to turn out well. Hear what Christ says,—"Ye are my friends, if ye do whatsoever I command you." If you do evil that good may come you cannot walk with him, but if your heart is set towards his statutes you shall find him loving you, and taking up his abode with you.

IV. Fourthly, by our text we are taught that THE MOST FRIENDLY ACTION A MAN CAN DO FOR JESUS IS TO OBEY HIM: "Ye are my friends, if ye do whatsoever I command you." Rich men have thought to do the most friendly act possible towards Christ by giving an immense sum to build a church, or to found almshouses or schools. If they are believers, and have done this thing as an act of obedience to Christ's law of stewardship, they have well done, and the more of such munificence the better, but where splendid benefactions are given out of ostentation, or from the idea that some merit will be gained by the consecration of a large amount of wealth, the whole business is unacceptable. If a man should give all the substance of his house for love it would utterly be contemned. Jesus asks not lavish expenditure, but ourselves. He has made this the token of true love: "If ye do whatsoever I command you." "To obey is better than sacrifice, and to hearken than the fat of rams." However much we are able to give we are bound to give it, and should give it cheerfully; but if we suppose that any amount of giving can stand as a substitute for personal obeying we are greatly mistaken. To bring our wealth and not to yield our hearts is to give the casket and steal the jewel. How dare we bring our sacrifice in a leprous hand? We must ourselves be cleansed in the atoning blood before we can be accepted, and our hearts must be changed before our offering can be pure in God's sight.

Others have imagined that they could show their friendliness to Christ by some remarkable action of self-mortification. Among Romanists, especially in the old time, it was believed that misery and merit went together, and so men tortured themselves that they might please God. They went for many a day without washing themselves or their clothes, and fancied that they thus acquired the odour of sanctity. I do not believe that Jesus thinks a man any more his friend because he is dirty. Some have put on a hair shirt, or have worn a chain girdle, which made raw wounds. I do not think that the kind Lord Jesus counts these things to be friendly acts. Ask any humane person whether he would be gratified by knowing that a friend wore a hair shirt for his sake, and he would answer, " Pray let the poor creature wear whatever is most comfortable to him, and that will please me best." The loving Jesus takes no delight in pain and discomfort : the maceration of the body is no doctrine of his. John the Baptist might be an ascetic, but certainly Jesus was not : he came eating and drinking, a man among men. He did not come to demand the rigours of a hermitage or a monastery, else he had never been seen at feasts. When we hear of the nuns of St. Ann sleeping bolt upright in their coffins, we take no particular satisfaction in their doing so ; a kind heart would beg them to go to bed. I went over a monastery some time ago, and over each bed was a little cat-o'-nine tails, which I sincerely hope was used to the satisfaction of the possessor, but I did not copy the idea, and buy a couple for my sons, neither have I sent one to each of my special friends, for I should never ask them to flog themselves as a proof of friendship. Our Lord cannot be gratified by self-inflicted, self-invented tortures. These things are will-worship, which is no worship. You may fast forty days if you like, but you will gain no merit by it. Jesus Christ has not demanded this as the gauge of friendship, neither will he regard us as his friends for this. He says, " Ye are my friends, if ye do whatsoever I command you," but he does not command you to starve, or to wear sackcloth, or to shut yourselves up in a cell : pride invents these things, but grace teaches obedience.

Certain persons have thought it would be the noblest form of holy service to enter into brotherhoods and sisterhoods. They fancied that they would be Christ's friends indeed if they joined " the Society of Jesus." I have sometimes asked myself whether it might not be well to form a league of Christian men all banded together, to live alone for Jesus, and to give themselves up entirely and wholly to his work ; but assuredly the formation of guilds, sisterhoods, or brotherhoods other than the great brotherhood of the church of God, is a thing never contemplated in the New Testament : you shall find no foreshadowing of Franciscans and Dominicans there. All godly women were sisters of mercy, and all Christlike men were of the Society of Jesus, but of monastic and conventual vows we read nothing. That which is not commanded in Scripture is superstition. We are to worship God according to *his* will, not according to our will ; and though I were to consecrate myself entirely to what Papists called the religious life, and get away from the associations of ordinary men, and try to spend my whole time in lonely contemplations, yet there would be nothing in it, because the Lord Jesus never required it at my hands. The thing that he does ask for is that we will do whatsoever he commands us. Why is it that people try to do something which he never did command ? A schoolmaster will suffer me to appeal to him on this point. If he said to a boy in the school, "Now is the time for you to take your slate and attend to arithmetic," and the boy instead fetched his copy-book, would he not ask if he had understood him? If after a few minutes he finds the boy writing does he say, " You have written that line very well ? " Not at all. It is small matter whether the writing be well or, ill done, for to be writing at all when he was told to be ciphering is a gross act of insubordination. So is it with you and me. We may do something else, and do it splendidly well, and other people may say, "What a pious man he is;" but if we do not the Lord's will we shall not be his friends. We may wear a piece of leather for a sandal, and brown serge for a garment, and forswear boots and coats, but there is no grace in apparel; excellence lies in doing what Christ has commanded.

Some think it a very friendly act towards Christ to attend many religious services in a consecrated building. They are at matins, and vespers, and feasts and fasts without number. Some of us prefer to have our religious services each day in our own homes, and it will be a dreadful thing when family prayer is given up for public services: but a number of people think little of family devotion, they must needs repair to the parish church or to some other temple made with hands; but let no man dream that Jesus is thus made our friend. We are not to forsake the assembling of ourselves together as the manner of some is, it is well to be f u nd meeting with God's people as often as we can; but still you may multiply your sacraments and increase your ceremonies, and you may attend to this service, and to the other service, until your heart is worn away with grinding at the mill of outward religion. Ye are Christ's friends, if ye do whatsoever he commands ye: that is a better test than early communion or daily mass.

It comes to this, dear friends, that we must steadily, carefully, persistently, cheerfully, do the will of God from the heart in daily life, from the first waking moment till our eyes are closed. Say concerning everything, "What would Jesus have me do about this? What is the teaching of Christ as to this?" "Whether ye eat or drink, or whatsoever ye do, do all in the name of the Lord Jesus, giving thanks unto God and the Father by him." You may be a domestic servant, and never be able to give a pound to church work, but you are Jesus' friend if you do whatsoever he commands you: you may be a housewife, and not able to do anything outside of the little family which requires all your attention, but if you are fulfilling your duty to your children, doing that which Christ commands you, you are among the friends of Jesus. You may be only a plain working-man, or a tradesman with a small shop; nobody hears of your name; but if you set the example of honesty, uprightness, and piety, doing all things as to Christ because he has saved you, he will call you his friend. What patent of nobility can equal this? Friendship with Christ is worth a thousand dukedoms.

The practical outcome of it all is this: examine every question as to duty by the light of this one enquiry :—Will this be a friendly action to Christ? If I do this shall I act as Christ's friend? Will my conduct honour him? Then I am glad. If it will dishonour him I will have nothing to do with it. Set each distinct action, as far as you are able, in the scales, and let this be the weight :—Is it a friendly action towards my Redeemer? I wish that we all lived as if Jesus were always present, as if we could see his wounds, and gaze into his lovely countenance. Suppose that to-morrow you are brought into temptation by being asked to do something questionable, decide it this way : if Jesus could come in at that moment and show you his hands and his feet, how would you act in his sight? Behave as you would act under the realised presence of the Well-beloved. You would not do anything unkind to him, would you? Certainly you would not do anything to grieve him if you saw him before your eyes. Well, keep him always before you. The psalmist cried, " I have set the Lord always before me."

You will want much of the Holy Spirit's anointing to do this. May God give it to you. Live, dear friends, as if Christ would come at once and detect you in the very act. Do that which you would not be ashamed of if the next instant you should see the Lord sitting on the throne of his glory, and calling you before his bar. Thus living, you shall delight yourself in the abundance of peace.

> " So shall your walk be close with God,
> Calm and serene your frame ;
> So purer light shall mark the road
> That leads you to the Lamb."

Obedience will gladden you with the blissful presence of your Lord, and in that presence you shall find fulness of joy. You shall be the envied of all wise men, for you shall be the beloved of the Lord ; and your pathway, if it be not always smooth, shall be always safe, for Jesus never leaves his friend, and he will never leave you, but he will keep you even to the end. May this be my happy case and yours. Amen.

Portion of Scripture read before Sermon—John xix.

Hymns from " Our Own Hymn Book"—915, 119 (Song II.), 646.

"At Thy Word"

"And Simon answering said unto him, Master, we have toiled all the night, and have taken nothing : nevertheless at thy word I will let down the net."—Luke v. 5.

How very much may simple obedience partake of the sublime ! Peter went to catch up the net, and let it down into the sea, and he said as naturally as possible, " *At thy word* I will let down the net"; but he was there and then appealing to one of the grandest principles which rules among intelligent beings, and to the strongest force which sways the universe :—" At thy word." Great God, it is " at thy word " that seraphs fly and cherubs bow ! Thine angels which excel in strength do thy commandments hearkening to the voice of thy word. " At thy word " space and time first came into existence, and all things else that are. " At thy word,"—here is the cause of causes, the beginning of the creation of God. " By the word of the Lord were the heavens made," and by that word was the present constitution of this round world settled as it stands. When the earth was formless and dark, thy voice, O Lord, was heard, saying, " Let there be light," and " at thy word " light leaped forth. " At thy word " day and night took up their places, and " at thy word " the waters were divided from the waters by the firmament of heaven. " At thy word " the dry land appeared, and the seas retired to their channels. " At thy word " the globe was mantled over with green, and vegetable life began. " At thy word " appeared the sun and moon and stars, " for signs, and for seasons, and for days, and years." " At thy word " the living creatures filled the sea, and air, and land, and man at last appeared. Of all this we are well assured, for by faith we know that the worlds were framed by the word of God. Acting in conformity with the word of our Lord we feel ourselves to be in order with all the forces of the universe, travelling on the main track of all real existence. Is not this a sublime condition, even though it be seen in the common deeds of our everyday life?

It is not in creation alone that the word of the Lord is supreme, but in providence too its majestic power is manifested, for the Lord upholdeth all things by the word of his power. Snow and vapour and stormy wind are all fulfilling his word. His word runneth very swiftly. When frost binds up the life-floods of the year the Lord sendeth forth his word and melteth them. Nature abides and moves by the word of the Lord. So, too, all matters of fact and history are beneath the supreme word. Jehovah stands the centre of all things, as Lord of all he abides at the saluting-point, and all the events of the ages come marching by at his word, bowing to his sovereign will. "At thy word," O God, kingdoms arise and empires flourish : "at thy word" races of men become dominant, and tread down their fellows : "at thy word" dynasties die, kingdoms crumble, mighty cities become a wilderness, and armies of men melt away like the hoarfrost of the morning. Despite the sin of man and the rage of devils, there is a sublime sense in which all things from the beginning, since Adam crossed the threshold of Eden even until now, have happened according to the purpose and will of the Lord of hosts. Prophecy utters her oracles, and history writes her pages, "at thy word," O Lord.

It is wonderful to think of the fisherman of Galilee letting down his net in perfect consonance with all the arrangements of the ages. His net obeys the law which regulates the spheres. His hand consciously does what Arcturus and Orion are doing without thought. This little bell on the Galilean lake rings out in harmony with the everlasting chimes. "At thy word," saith Peter, as he promptly obeys, therein repeating the watchword of seas and stars, of winds and worlds. It is glorious thus to be keeping step with the marchings of the armies of the King of kings.

There is another way of working out this thought. "At thy word" has been the password of all good men from the beginning until now. Saints have acted upon these three words and found their marching orders in them. An ark is builded on dry land, and the ribald crowd gather about the hoary patriarch, laughing at him ; but he is not ashamed: for lifting his face to heaven he saith, "I have builded this great vessel, O Jehovah, at thy word." Abraham quits the place of his childhood, leaves his family, and goes with Sarah to a land of which he knows nothing, crossing the broad Euphrates, and entering upon a country possessed by the Canaanite, in which he roams as a stranger and a sojourner all his days. He dwells in tents with Isaac and Jacob. If any scoff at him for thus renouncing the comforts of settled life he lifts also his calm face to heaven and smilingly answers to the Lord, "It is at thy word." Ay, and even when his brow is furrowed, and the hot tear is ready to force itself from beneath the patriarch's eyelid, as he lifts his hand with the knife to stab Isaac to the heart, if any charge him with murder, or think him mad, he lifts the same placid face towards the majesty of the Most High and saith, "It is at thy word." At that word he joyfully sheathes the sacrificial knife, for he has proved his willingness to go to the utmost at the word of the Lord his God. If I were to introduce you to a thousand of the faithful ones who have shown the obedience of faith, in every case they would justify their acts by telling you that they did them "at God's word." Moses lifts his rod in the presence of the haughty Pharaoh, "at thy word," great God ! Nor does he lift that rod in vain at Jehovah's word, for thick and heavy fall the plagues upon the children of Ham. They are made to know that God's word returneth not to him void, but fulfilleth his purpose, whether it be of threatening or of promise. See Moses lead the people out of Egypt, the whole host in its myriads ! Mark how he has brought them to the Red Sea, where the wilderness doth shut them in. The heights frown on either side, and the rattle of Egypt's war-chariots is behind. How came Moses so to play the fool and bring them here? Were there no graves in Egypt that thus he brought them forth to die on the Red Sea shore? The answer of Moses is the quiet reflection that he did it at Jehovah's word, and God justifies that word, for the sea opens wide a highway for the elect of God, and they march joyfully through, and with timbrels and dances on the other side they sing unto the Lord who hath triumphed gloriously. If in after days you find Joshua compassing Jericho, and not assailing it with battering rams, but only with one great blast of trumpets, his reason is that God has spoken to him by his word. And so right on, for time would fail me to speak of Samson, and Jephthah, and Barak : these men did what they did at God's word ; and doing it, the Lord was with them. Is it bringing things down from the sublime to the ridiculous to talk of Peter and the net which he casts over the side of his little boat? Oh, no. We are ourselves ridiculous when we do not make our own lives sublime by the obedience of faith. Certainly, there may be as much sublimity in casting a net as in building an ark, lifting a rod, or sounding a ram's horn ; and it is clear that if it be done in faith, the simplest action of life may be sublimely great. The flash of the wave as it covers Peter's net may be as sublime before the Lord as the glory of the Red Sea billow when it returned in its strength. God who sees a world in a drop sees wonders in the smallest act of faith. Do not, I pray you, think that sublimity lies in masses, to be measured by a scale, so that a mile shall be sublime and an inch shall be absurd. We measure not morals and spirituals by rods and chains. The common act of fishing at Christ's word links Peter with all the principalities, and powers, and forces which in all ages have known this as their only law,—" He spake, and it was done; he commanded, and it stood fast." We too shall have fellowship with the sublime if we know how to be perfectly obedient to the word of the Lord.

This ought to be the rule of all Christians for the whole of their lives, —" At thy word." This should direct us in the church and in the world ; it should guide us in our spiritual beliefs and in our secular acts, " At thy word." I wish it were so. We hear boastings that the Bible, and the Bible alone, is the religion of Protestants. It is a mere boast. Few Protestants can honestly repeat the assertion. They have other books to which they pay deference, and other rules, and other guides, beyond, and above, and even in opposition to, the one Word of God. It ought not to be so. The power of the church and the power of the individual to please God shall never be fully known till we get back to the simple yet sublime rule of our text, " At thy word."

I am just going to hammer upon that phrase this morning as God shall help me : " At thy word." This rule has many applications. First, I shall somewhat repeat myself by saying that *it ought to apply to the affairs of ordinary life ;* secondly, *it should apply to matters of spiritual profiting ;* and thirdly, and here I shall enlarge, *it ought to find its chief application in our great life business, which is being fishers of men.*

I. " At thy word" should apply TO ALL THE AFFAIRS OF ORDINARY LIFE. I mean, first, as to continuance in honest industry. " Let every man abide in the same calling wherein he was called." Many a man in the present trying crisis is half ready to throw up his work, and run away from his business, because he has toiled all night and taken nothing. Truly, the financial darkness has lasted long, and does not yet yield to the dawning, but yet Christians must not murmur or leave their posts. Oh tried ones, continue to be diligent in your business, still provide things honest in the sight of all men. Labour on in hope. Say just as Peter did, "Nevertheless at thy word I will let down the net." "Except the Lord build the house, they labour in vain that build it:" you know that truth full well; know this also, that the Lord will not forsake his people. Your best endeavours will not of themselves bring you prosperity; still, do not relax those endeavours. As God's word to you is to quit yourselves like men, and be strong, gird up the loins of your mind, be sober, and stand fast. Throw not away your shield, cast not away your confidence, but stand steadily in your rank till the tide of battle turns. God has placed you where you are, move not till his providence calls you. Do not run before the cloud. Take down the shutters to-morrow morning, and display your goods, and let not despondency drive you to anything that is rash or unseemly. Say, "Nevertheless at thy word I will let down the net."

If I am speaking to those who are out of work just now, searching for some place where they can provide bread for themselves and for their families, as is their duty, let them hear, and ponder. If any man does not do his best to provide for his own household he comes not under a gospel blessing, but he is said to be worse than a heathen man and a publican,—it is the duty of us all to labour with our hands that which is good, that we may have to give to the needy as well as to those dependent on us. If after having gone about this city till your feet are blistered you can find nothing to do, do not sit at home next Monday sulkily saying, "I will not try again." Apply my text to this painful trial, and yet again sally forth in hope, saying with Peter, "We have toiled all the night, and have taken nothing: nevertheless at thy word I will let down the net." Let men see that a Christian is not readily driven to despair: nay, let them see that when the yoke is made more heavy the Lord has a secret way of strengthening the backs of his children to bear their burdens. If the Holy Spirit shall make you calmly resolute you will honour God much more by your happy perseverance than the talkative by his fine speeches, or the formalist by his outward show. Common life is the true place in which to prove the truth of godliness and bring glory to God. Not by doing extraordinary works, but by the piety of ordinary life is the Christian known and his religion honoured. At God's word hold on even to the end. "Trust in the Lord, and do good; so shalt thou dwell in the land, and verily thou shalt be fed."

It may be, too, that you have been endeavouring in your daily life to acquire skill in your business, and you have not succeeded, or you have tried to acquire more knowledge, so that you could better fulfil your vocation, but hitherto you have not prospered as you could wish. Do not, therefore, cease from your efforts. Christians must never be idlers. Our Lord Jesus would never have it said that his disciples are a sort of cowards who, if they do not succeed the first time, will never try again. We are to be patterns of all the moral virtues as well as of the spiritual graces: therefore, at the bidding of the Lord, work on with mind and hand, and look to him for the blessing. "At his word" let down the net once more: he may intend largely to bless you when by trial you have been prepared to bear the benediction.

This will apply very closely to those who are labouring hard in the training of children. It may be that with your own children you may not have succeeded yet: the boy's spirit may still be wild and proud, and the girl may not yet have yielded to obedience and submission. Or you may be working in the Sunday-school, or in the day-school, trying to impart knowledge, and to fashion the youthful mind aright, and you may have been baffled; but if it is your business to teach, do not be overcome. Stand to your work as though you heard Jesus say, "Whatsoever ye do, do it heartily, as unto the Lord, and not unto men." Earnestly, then, at his word again let down the net.

I counsel you, dear friends, in everything to which you set your hands, if it be a good thing, do it with all your might; and if it be not a good thing, have nothing to do with it. It may be possible that you are called to teach the age some moral truth. In most generations individuals have been called to carry out reforms, and to promote progress. You are bound to love your neighbour as yourself, therefore as you have opportunity do good unto all men. If you have tried, and hitherto have not won a hearing, do not give up your point; if it is a good thing, and you are a Christian man, never let it be said that you were afraid or ashamed. I admire in Palissy the potter, not only his Christianity, which could not be overcome by persecution, but his perseverance in his own business of making pottery. His last farthing and his last breath would have gone in discovering a glaze, or bringing out a colour. I love to see such men believers. I should not like to see our Lord followed by a set of cowards who could not fight the common battles of life: how should such as these become worthy of the lordlier chivalry which wrestles with spiritual wickedness in high places? It is for us to be bravest among the brave in the plains of common life, that when we are summoned to higher fields, where still greater deeds are needed, we may go there trained for the higher service.

Does it seem to you to be a little out of place to be talking thus from the pulpit? I do not think so. I notice how in the Old Testament we are told of the sheep and the cattle, and the fields and the harvests of good men; and these had to do with their religion. I notice how the prudent woman according to Solomon looked well to her household; and I observe that we have in the Bible a book of Proverbs, and another called Ecclesiastes, with little spiritual teaching in them, but a great deal of good, sound, practical common sense. It is evident to me that the Lord intends that our faith should not be penned up in a pew, but should walk the shop, and be seen in every walk of life. The great principle of my text fell from the lips of a working man, and to the working man I return it: it was connected with a net and a boat, the implements of his labour, and with these common things I would link it; and I would say to all who serve the Lord, in this present evil world,—in the name of God, if you have anything to do, be not so desponding and despairing as to cease from it, but, according to his word, once more go forward in your honest endeavours, and, like Peter, say, "I will let down the net." This may prove a word in season to some who are weary of the hardness of the times. I shall rejoice if it nerves an arm or cheers a heart. Have faith in God, my tried brethren. "Be ye steadfast, unmoveable, always abounding in the work of the Lord."

II. IN MATTERS OF SPIRITUAL PROFITING we must at the word of Christ let down the net again. I put this, first, to those who have been up to this Tabernacle a great many times, heartily, if I am to believe them, *hoping to find salvation.* You have prayed before the sermon began that the Lord would really bless the sermon to you. Now, mark, I do not understand you at all; I cannot make you out; because the way of salvation is open to you at this very moment, and it is, "Believe on the Lord Jesus Christ, and thou shalt be saved." You have nothing to wait for, and all your waiting is sinful. If you say you are waiting for the stirring of the pool, I tell you there is no pool to be stirred, and no angel to stir it. That pool was dried up long ago, and angels never go that way now. Our Lord Jesus Christ shut up Bethesda when he came, and said to the man lying there, "Rise, take up thy bed, and walk." That is what he says to you. You have no business waiting; but as you are, and are here this morning, I would earnestly invite you at the word of Christ, who has bidden us preach the gospel to every creature—"believe and live." Let down the net once more, and let it down this way; say, "My Lord, I believe; help thou mine unbelief." Breathe a prayer now to Jesus that he would accept you. Submit yourself to him, and beseech him to become now at this moment your Saviour. You will be heard. Plenty of fish are waiting to be taken in the net of faith. At the Lord's word let it down.

But I will now speak to others present, who have been letting down their nets, in vain, perhaps, in the form of *importunate prayer.* Have you been praying for the conversion of a relative, or pleading for some other good thing which you believe to be according to the will of God, and after long pleading—pleading in the night, for your spirit has been sad—are you tempted never to offer that petition any more? Now then, at Christ's word, who said that men ought always to pray and not to faint,—at Christ's word, who says, "Pray without ceasing," let down the net, and pray again. Not because the circumstances which surround you are more favourable, but simply because Jesus bids you, continue in prayer; and who knows but that this very time you will meet with success!

Or have you been *searching the Scriptures to find a promise* which will suit your case? Do you want to get hold of some good word from God that will cheer you? Shoals of such fish are around your boat; the sea of Scripture is full of them: fish of promise, I mean, but, alas! you cannot catch one of them. Nevertheless, try again. Go home this afternoon, and search the Scriptures again with prayer, and beseech the Holy Spirit to apply a precious portion to your heart, that you may by faith enjoy the sweetness of it; and who knows but you shall this very day obtain your desire, and receive a larger blessing than your mind can fully contain, so that in your case also the net shall break through the fulness of the favour.

Or it may be you have been labouring a long while after *some holy attainment;* you want to conquer a besetting sin, to exercise firmer faith, to exhibit more zeal, and to be more useful, but you have not yet gained your desire. Now, then, since it is the Lord's mind that you should be "perfect in every good work to do his will," do not cease from your purpose, but at his word let down your net again. Never despair. That temper of yours will be conquered yet; that unbelief of yours will give way to holy faith. Let down the net, and all the graces may yet be taken in it, to be yours for the rest of your life. Only at Christ's word still labour for the best things, and he will give them to you.

Or are you seeking just now *the closer presence of Christ,* and a nearer fellowship with him ? Are you yearning after a sight of his face—that face which doth outshine the morning ? Do you wish to be brought into his banqueting-house to be satiated with his love ? And have you cried in vain ? Then cry once more, " at his word," for he bids you come to him: his loving voice invites you to draw near. At his word press forward once again, let down the net once more, and joys await you unspeakable, surpassing all you have hitherto experienced.

Thus you see that there is a just application of the great principle of the text to our spiritual profiting. God help us by his gracious Spirit to carry it out from day to day.

III. The great principle of our text should be applied to OUR LIFE-BUSINESS. And what is the life-business of every Christian here ? Is it not soul-winning ? That we may glorify God by the bringing of others to the faith of Christ is the great object of our remaining here on earth : otherwise we should have been caught up to swell the harmony of the heavenly songs. It is expedient for many wandering sheep here below that we should tarry here till we have brought them home to the great Shepherd and Bishop of souls.

Our way of winning men for Christ, or, to use his own metaphor, our method of catching men, is by letting down the net of the gospel. We have learned no other way of holy fishery. Men with great zeal and little knowledge are inventing ingenious methods for catching men, but for my part I believe in nothing but letting down the gospel net, by telling out the story of the love of God to men in Christ Jesus. No new gospel has been committed to us by Jesus, and he has authorized no new way of making it known. Our Lord has called all of us to the work of proclaiming free pardon through his blood to all who believe in him. Each believer has a warrant to seek the conversion of his fellows. May not every man seek to save his brother from the burning ? Must not Jesus smile on any man's endeavour to deliver his neighbour from going down to eternal death ? Has he not said, " Let him that heareth say, Come"? Whosoever hears the gospel is to invite others to come to Christ. The word of the Lord is our warrant for keeping to our one work of making known the gospel : it would be a sorry act of mutiny if we were either to be silent, or to preach another gospel which is not another. The word of the Lord is a warrant which justifies the man who obeys it. "Where the word of a king is there is power." What higher authority can we need ? "Oh, but," they say, " you ought to advance to something higher than the mere elementary doctrine of grace, and give the people something more in keeping with the progress of the period." We shall not do so while Jesus bids us go into all the world and preach the gospel to every creature. If we do what he bids us the responsibility of the matter rests no longer with us. Whatever comes of it we are clear if we have obeyed orders. A servant is not to justify his master's message, but to deliver it. This makes it a joy to preach, this doing it "at thy word." Our business is to do what Christ tells us, as Christ tells us, and to do this again and again, so long as we have breath in our bodies. The commanding word cries ever to us, "Preach the gospel, preach the gospel to every creature!" Our justification for setting forth Christ crucified, and incessantly bidding men believe and live, lies in that same word which bade Peter walk the sea, and bade Moses fetch water out of a rock.

The result of this preaching will justify him who commanded it. No man at the last will be able to say to the Saviour, "You set your servants an impossible task, and you gave them an instrument to wield which was not at all adapted to produce its end." No, but at the closing up of all things it shall be seen that for the salvation of the elect there was nothing better than a crucified Saviour, and to make that crucified Saviour known there was no better means than the simple proclamation of his word by honest lips in the power of the Spirit of the Lord. The foolishness of preaching will turn out to be the great proof of the wisdom of God. Brethren, you that teach in the school, or you that preach from the pulpit, or distribute tracts, or speak personally to individuals, you need not be afraid but what wisdom will exonerate herself from all charges, and vindicate her own methods. You may be called a fool to-day for preaching the gospel, but that accusation, like rust on a sword, will wear off as you use the weapon in the wars of the Lord. The preaching of the word soon puts down all clamours against itself: those clamours mainly arise because it is not preached. No one calls the gospel effete where it is smiting right and left like a great two-handed sword. Our reply to the outcry about the failure of the pulpit is to get into it and preach with the Holy Ghost sent down from heaven.

Indeed, this word of Christ, whereby he gives us his warrant for letting down the net, is such that it amounts to a command, and it will leave us guilty if we do not obey. Suppose Simon Peter had said, "We have toiled all the night, and have taken nothing; and therefore, notwithstanding thy word, I will not let down the net"? Then Simon Peter had been guilty of disobedience to his Lord, and blasphemy against the Son of God. What shall I say to any of my fellow-Christians who profess to be called of God, and to be Christ's disciples, and yet never do let down the net? Is it so that you are doing nothing for the truth? that you never disseminate the gospel? Is it so that you call yourselves lights of the world, and yet never shine? that you are sowers of the seed, and yet forget that you have a seed-basket? Am I addressing any members of this church who are in this respect wasting their lives? Is it so that it is professedly your life's object to be fishers of men, and yet you have never cast a net, nor even helped to draw one on shore? Are you dwelling among us under false pretences? Are you mocking God by a fruitless profession which you never try to make fruitful? I have not the strength with which to condemn you, but I would to God your own conscience might fulfil that office. What shall be said of the man to whom the Lord gives it in charge that he shall make known the glad tidings of salvation from eternal misery, and yet he is sinfully silent? The great Physician has entrusted you with the medicine which heals the sick; you see them die about you, but you never speak of the remedy! The great King has given you the meal with which to feed the hungry, and you lock the storehouse door, while the crowds are starving in your streets. Is not this a crime which may well make a man of God weep over you? This great London of ours is growing heathenish to the very core, and yet our Lord has given the gospel into the hands of his churches; what can be the reason of the indifference of the godly? If we keep this gospel to ourselves, verily coming ages will condemn us as cruel to our posterity. Succeeding generations will point to our era, and say, "What sort of men were these, that had the light, and shut it up in a dark lantern?" In a century to come, when others shall stand in this city, and walk these streets, they will say, "A curse upon the memory of the ministers and people who failed in their duty, who came to the kingdom in a solemn time, but never realized their calling, and so missed the end and object of their being!" May we be spared from such a calamity as this. Yes, we have a warrant for labouring to spread the truth of God, and more than a warrant; we have a statute from the throne, a peremptory command, and it is woe to us if we preach not the gospel.

Now, brethren, this warrant from Christ is one which, if we be in the state of heart of Simon Peter, will be omnipotent with us this morning. It was very powerful with Simon Peter. For, observe, he was *under the influence of a great disappointment*, yet he let down the net. "We have toiled all the night." Some say, "We have had all this gospel preaching, we have had all these revivals, all these stirs, and nothing has come of it." When was that? I hear a good deal of this talk, but what are the facts? "Oh," you say, "you know we have had a great deal of revival a little while ago." I do not know anything of the sort. We have had flashes of light here and there, but comparatively so little that it is a pity to make so much of it. Moreover, considering the little that has ever been done for it, the spread of the gospel has been marvellous. Look at gospel-work at the present moment in India! People say that the Christian faith is not spreading. I say that it is spreading wonderfully as compared with the labour expended and the sacrifice made. If in that land you spend a penny and get a thousand pounds, you have no right to say, "What is that? We want a million." If your desires are thus exacting, prove their sincerity by corresponding action. Increase your outlay. The harvest is wonderful considering the little seed, but if you wish for more sheaves sow more. The church has had an enormous return for what little she has done. In England there have been partial revivals, but to what have they amounted? A flash of light has been seen in a certain district, but darkness has still remained supreme over the length and breadth of the country. The papers have reported a great work in a certain spot, but if the papers had reported the places wherein there has been no revival we should have had a different view of things! A little corner at the top of a column would have sufficed for the good, and column after column would not have sufficed to make known the black side of the situation. The fact is the church has scarcely ever been in a state of universal revival since the day of Pentecost. There has been a partial moving among Christians every now and then, but the whole mass throughout has never burned and flamed with the earnestness which the grand cause demands. Oh, that the Lord would set the whole church on fire ! We have no cause whatever for disappointment. In proportion to the little effort put out great things have come to us ; therefore let us get to our nets again, and say no more about the night in which we have toiled.

But next, this command in Peter *overcame his love of ease* Evidently he was tired when he said, "We have toiled all the night." Fishing is hard work, especially when no fish are caught. It is natural to wish to be excused from further toil when you are already weary with unrewarded labour. I have heard some Christians say, "You know I had my time in the Sunday school years ago, and then I used to work too much for my strength." No doubt their efforts were stupendous in the remote ages of their youthful zeal ; we can hardly imagine what they must have been like, for no relic remains to assist our conceptions. At this time they feel authorized to take things easy, for they owe no more to their Lord, or at least they do not intend to pay any more. Is it so that any one of us can cease from service when it is plain that we do not cease from receiving mercy at the Lord's hands ? Are we not ashamed of the case when it is plainly put ? "Take it easy." Yes, soon, very soon, we shall take it easy, for there will be rest enough in the grave. Just now, while souls of men are perishing, to relax our efforts is wickedness. No, no, Peter, although you may be now in a dripping sweat through having toiled all night, you must get at it again. He does so. The night's work is nothing, he must work in the day too, if he is to catch fish.

Moreover, the command of Christ was so supreme over Peter that he was *not held back by carnal reason,* for reason would say "If you could not catch fish in the night you will certainly not do so in the day." Night was the special time for taking fish on the Gennesaret lake, and by day, when the garish sun was lighting up the waves, and letting the fish see every single mesh of the net, they were not likely to come into it ; but when Christ commands, the most unlikely time is likely, and the most unpromising sphere becomes hopeful. No act is out of season when Christ commands it. If he says, "go," go at once, without deliberation. Say not "There are yet four months, and then cometh harvest." "The fields are white already to the harvest." Peter lets down the net at once, and wisely does he act at Christ's word.

The lesson to you and to me is this : Let us do as Peter did, and let down the net *personally,* for the apostle said, "I will let down the net." Brother, cannot you do something yourself with your own heart, lips, and hands ? Sister, cannot you do something yourself with your own gentle spirit ? "I was thinking about getting half a dozen friends to form a committee to relieve the poor around us." Nothing will ever come of it : the poor will not get a basin of soup or a hunch of bread. Set about it yourself. "But I think I might get a dozen to come together, and organize a society." Yes, and then move resolutions and amendments all day long, and finish up with passing votes of mutual approbation. You had better get to work yourself as Peter did.

And you had better do it *at once,* for Peter immediately let down the net, as soon as ever he had launched out into the deep. You may never have another opportunity ; your zeal may have evaporated, or your life may be over. Peter, however, only let down one net, and there was the pity of it. If John and James and all the rest had let down their nets, the result would have been much better. " Why ? " say you. Because, through there being only one net, that net was overstrained, and broke. If all the nets had been used, they might taken more fish, and no net would have been broken. I was reading some time ago of a take of mackerel at Brighton ; when the net was full, the mackerel sticking in all the meshes made it so heavy that the fishermen could not raise it, and the boat itself was in some danger of going down, so that they had to cut away the net and lose the fish. Had there been many nets and boats they might have buoyed up the whole of the fish ; and so they might have done in this case. As it was, many fish were lost through the breaking of the net. If a church can be so awakened that each individual gets to work in the power of the Holy Spirit, and all the individuals combine, then how many souls will be captured for Jesus! Multitudes of souls are lost to the blessed gospel because of our broken nets, and the net gets broken because we are not well united in the holy service, and by our unwisdom cause loss to our Master's cause. Ministers need not become worn out with labour if all would take their share : one boat would not begin to sink if the other boats took a part of the blessed load.

Now, brothers and sisters, I close by saying that if I have accomplished anything this morning by the help of God's Spirit, I hope I have made you ready to accept the following directory of service drawn from the text. The way in which to serve God is to do it at his word. I pray that none of us may sink into serving the Lord as a matter of routine. May we never fall to serving him in our own strength. We must preach, teach, and labour in his name, because we hear him bidding us do it. We must act at his word. If this were the case we should work with much more faith, with much more earnestness, and with much more likelihood of success. It is a blessed thing to see Christ sitting in the boat while you cast out the net. If you catch a glimpse of his approving smile as he watches you, you will work right heartily. We must labour in entire dependence upon him, not preaching or teaching because in our judgment it is the right thing to do,—Peter did not think so,—but because Jesus gives the word, and his word is law. You may not work because you have any expectation of success from the excellence of your work, or from the nature of the people among whom you labour, but because Jesus has given you the word. You stand there doing a thing which critics sneer at as absurd, but you do it in all confidence, believing that it must be wise, because Jesus bids you do it. I remember well how some of our brethren used to talk to us. They said, " You preach the gospel to dead sinners ; you bid them repent and believe. You might just as well shake a pocket-handkerchief over a grave and bid the corpse come out of it." Exactly so. They spoke the truth, but then I would delight to go and shake a pocket-handkerchief over graves and bid the dead live if Jesus bade me do so. I should expect to see the cemetery crack and heave from end to end if I were sent on such an errand by the Lord. I would accept the duty joyfully. The more absurd the wise men of our age make the gospel out to be, and the more they show that it is powerless to produce the end designed, the more will we persevere in our old method of preaching Jesus crucified. Our resolves are not to be shaken by that mode of reasoning. We never did draw our argument for preaching the gospel from the work itself, but from the orders given us to do it, and we would rather be acting upon the responsibility of Christ than upon our own. I would rather be a fool and do what Christ tells me, than be the wisest man of the modern school, and despise the word of the Lord. I would rather lay the responsibility of my life at the feet of him who bids me live according to his word than seek out an object in life for myself, and feel that the responsibility rested on my own shoulders. Let us be willing to be under orders to Christ, willing to persevere under difficulties, willing to begin anew in his service from this very hour. Amen.

PORTION OF SCRIPTURE READ BEFORE SERMON—Luke v. 1—26.

Elijah's Plea

"Let it be known that I have done all these things at thy word."—1 Kings xviii. 36.

THE acts of Elijah were very singular. It had not been known from the foundations of the earth that a man should shut up the doors of the rain for the space of three years. Yet Elijah suddenly leaped upon the scene, announced the judgment of the Lord, and then disappeared for a time. When he reappears, at the bidding of God, he orders Ahab to gather the priests of Baal; and to put to the test the question as to whether Baal or Jehovah was indeed God. Bullocks shall be slain and laid upon the wood without fire; and the God who shall answer by fire shall be determined to be the one living and true God, the God of Israel. We might question within ourselves what right the prophet had to restrain the clouds, or to put God's honour under test. Suppose the Lord had not willed to answer him by fire; had he any right to make the glory of God hang upon such terms as he proposed? The answer is that *he had done all these things according to God's word.* It was no whim of his to chastise the nation with a drought. It was no scheme of his, concocted in his own brain, that he should put the Godhead of Jehovah or of Baal to the test by a sacrifice to be consumed by miraculous fire. Oh, no! If you read the life of Elijah through, you will see that whenever he takes a step it is preceded by, "the word of the Lord came unto Elijah the Tishbite." He never acts of himself; God is at his back. He moves according to the divine will, and he speaks according to the divine teaching; and he pleads this with the Most High,—"I have done all these things at thy word; now let it be known that it is so." It makes the character of Elijah stand out, not as an example of reckless daring, but as the example of a man of sound mind. Faith in God is true wisdom: childlike confidence in the word of God is the highest form of common-sense. To believe him that cannot lie, and trust in him that cannot fail, is a kind of wisdom that none but fools will laugh at. The wisest of men must concur in the opinion that it is always best to place your reliance where it will certainly be justified, and always best to believe that which cannot possibly be false.

Elijah had so believed, and acted on his belief, and now he naturally expects to be justified in what he has done. An ambassador never dreams that his authorized acts will be repudiated by his king. If a man acts as your agent and does your bidding, the responsibility of his acts lies with you, and you must back him up. It were, indeed, an atrocious thing to send a servant on an errand, and, when he faithfully performed it to the letter, to repudiate your sending him. It is not so with God. If we will only so trust him as to do as he bids us, he will never fail us ; but he will see us through, though earth and hell should stand in the way. It may not be to-day, nor to-morrow, but as surely as the Lord liveth, the time shall come when he that trusted him shall have joy of his confidence.

It seems to me that Elijah's plea is to obedient saints *a firm ground for prayer,* and to those who cannot say that they have acted according to God's word, it is *a solemn matter for question.*

I. To begin with, this is A FIRM GROUND FOR PRAYER. You are *a minister of God, or a worker in the cause of Christ,* and you go forth and preach the gospel with many tears and prayers, and you continue to use all means, such as Christ has ordained : do you say to yourself, "May I expect to have fruit of all this ?" Of course you may. You are not sent on a frivolous errand : you are not bidden to sow dead seed that will never spring up. But when that anxiety weighs heavily upon your heart, go you to the mercy-seat with this as one of your arguments, "Lord, I have done according to thy word. Now let it be seen that it is even so. I have preached thy word, and thou hast said, ' It shall not return unto me void.' I have prayed for these people, and thou hast said, ' The effectual fervent prayer of a righteous man availeth much'; let it be seen that this is according to thy word." Or, if you are a teacher, you can say, " I brought my children in supplication before thee, and I have gone forth, after studying thy Word, to teach them, to the best of my ability, the way of salvation. Now, Lord, I claim it of thy truth that thou shouldest justify my teaching, and my expectation, by giving me to see the souls of my children saved by thee, through Jesus Christ, thy Son." Do you not see that you have a good argument, if the Lord has set you to do this work ? He has, as it were, bound himself by that very fact to support you in the doing of it ; and if you, with holy diligence and carefulness, do all these things according to his word, then you may come with certainty to the throne of grace, and say unto him, " Do as thou hast said. Hast thou not said, ' He that goeth forth and weepeth, bearing precious seed, shall doubtless come again with rejoicing, bringing his sheaves with him' ? Lord I have done that. Give me my sheaves. Thou has said, ' Cast thy bread upon the waters, for thou shalt find it after many days.' Lord, I have done that ; and therefore I entreat thee fulfil thy promise to me." You may plead in this fashion with the same boldness which made Elias say in the presence of all the people, " Let it be known this day that thou art God in Israel, and that I have done all these things at thy word."

Next, I would apply this teaching *to a whole church.* I am afraid many churches of Christ are not prospering. The congregations are thin, the church is diminishing, the prayer-meeting scantily attended, spiritual life low. If I can conceive of a church in such a condition which, nevertheless, can say to God, "We have done all these things at thy word," I should expect to see that church soon revived in answer to prayer. The reason why some churches do not prosper is, because they have *not* done according to God's word. They have not even cared to know what God's Word says. Another book is their standard. A man is their leader and legislator, instead of the inspired Word of God. Some churches are doing little or nothing for the conversion of sinners. But any man, in any church, who can go before God, and say, " Lord, we have had among us the preaching of the gospel ; and we have earnestly prayed for the blessing ; we have gathered about thy minister, and we have held him up in the arms of prayer and faith ; we have, as individual Christians, sought out each one his particular service, we have gone forth each one to bring in souls to thee, and we have lived in godliness of life by the help of thy grace, now, therefore prosper thy cause," shall find it a good plea. Real prosperity must come to any church that walks according to Christ's rules, obeys Christ's teaching, and is filled with Christ's Spirit. I would exhort all members of churches that are in a poor way just now, to see to it that all things are done at God's word, and then hopefully wait in holy confidence. The fire from heaven must come : the blessing cannot be withheld.

The same principle may be applied also *to any individual believers* who are in trouble through having done right. It happens often that a man feels, "I could make money, but I must not ; for the course proposed would be wrong. Such a situation is open, but it involves what my conscience does not approve. I will rather suffer than I will make gain by doing anything that is questionable." It may be that you are in great trouble distinctly through obedience to God. Then, you are the man above all others who may lay this case before the Most High : " Lord, I have done all these things at thy word, and thou hast said, ' I will never leave thee nor forsake thee.' I beseech thee interpose for me." Somehow or other God will provide for you. If he means you to be further tried, he will give you strength to bear it ; but the probabilities are that now he has tested you, he will bring you forth from the fire as gold.

> "Do good and know no fear,
> For so thou in the land shalt dwell,
> And God thy food prepare."

Once again. I would like to apply this principle *to the seeking sinner.* You are anxious to be saved. You are attentive to the word, and your heart says, " Let me know what this salvation is, and how to come at it, for I will have it whatever stands in the way." You have heard Jesus say, " Strive to enter in at the strait gate." You have heard his bidding, " Labour not for the meat which perisheth, but for that which endureth to life eternal." You long to enter the strait gate, and eat of the meat which endureth ; you would give worlds for such a boon. Thou hast well spoken, my friend. Now, listen:—thou canst not have heaven through thy doings, as a matter of merit. There is no merit possible to thee, for thou hast sinned, and art already condemned. But God has laid down certain lines upon which he has promised to meet thee, and to bless thee. Hast thou followed those lines ? For if thou hast, he will not be false to thee. It is written,—" He that believeth and is baptized shall be saved"—can you come before God, and say, "I have believed and have been baptized"? then you are on firm pleading ground. It is written again,—" Whoso confesseth and forsaketh his sins shall have mercy." When you have confessed them, and forsaken them, you have a just claim upon the promise of God, and you can say to him, "Lord, fulfil this word unto thy servant, upon which thou hast caused me to hope. There is no merit in my faith, or my baptism, or my repentance, or my forsaking of sin; yet as thou hast put thy promise side by side with these things, and I have been obedient to thee therein, I now come to thee, and say, ' Prove thine own truth, for I have done all these things at thy word.'" No sinner will come before God at last, and say, "I trusted as thou didst bid me trust; and yet I am lost." It is impossible. Thy blood, if thou art lost, will be on thine own head; but thou shalt never be able to lay thy soul's damnation at the door of God. *He* is not false : it is *thou* that art false.

You see, then, how the principle can be applied in prayer : "I have done these things at thy word ; therefore, O Lord, do as thou hast said."

II. We shall go a little over the same ground while I ask you to put yourselves through your paces by way of SELF-EXAMINATION as to whether or not you have done all these things at God's word.

First, let every *worker* here who has not been successful answer this question—Have you done all these things at God's word? Come. *Have you preached the gospel ?* Was it the gospel ? Was it Christ you preached, or merely something about Christ ? Come. Did you give the people bread, or did you give them plates to put the bread on, and knives to cut the bread with ? Did you give them drink, or did you give them the cup that had been near the water ? Some preaching is not gospel ; it is a knife that smells of the cheese, but it is not cheese. See to that matter.

If you preached the gospel, *did you preach it rightly ?* That is to say, did you state it affectionately, earnestly, clearly, plainly ? If you preach the gospel in Latinized language, the common people will not know what it means ; and if you use great big academy words and dictionary words, the market people will be lost while they are trying to find out what you are at. You cannot expect God to bless you unless the gospel is preached in a very simple way. Have you preached the truth lovingly, with all your heart, throwing your very self into it, as if beyond everything you desired the conversion of those you taught? Has prayer been mixed with it? Have you gone into the pulpit without prayer? Have you come out of it without prayer ? Have you been to the Sabbath-school without prayer ? Have you come away from it without prayer ? If so, since you failed to ask for the blessing, you must not wonder if you do not get it.

And another question—*Has there been an example to back your teaching ?* Brethren, have we lived as we have preached ? Sisters, have you lived as you have taught in your classes ? These are questions we ought to answer, because perhaps God can reply to us, "No, you have not done according to my word. It was not my gospel you preached : you were a thinker, and you thought out your own thoughts, and I never promised to bless your thoughts, but only my revealed truth. You spoke without affection; you tried to glorify yourself by your oratory; you did not care whether souls were saved or not." Or suppose that God can point to you, and say, "Your example was contrary to your teaching. You looked one way, but you pulled another way." Then there is no plea in prayer: is there ? Come, let us alter. Let us try to rise to the highest pitch of obedience by the help of God's Spirit: not that we can merit success, but that we can command it if we do but act according to God's bidding. Paul planteth, and Apollos watereth, and God giveth the increase.

And now let me turn to *a church*, and put questions to that church. A certain church does not prosper. I wish that every church would let this question go through all its membership: do we as a church acknowledge the headship of Christ ? Do we acknowledge the Statute-Book of Christ—the one Book which alone and by itself is the religion of a Christian man ? Do we as a church seek the glory of God ? Is that our main and only object ? Are we travailing in birth for the souls of the people that live near us ? Are we using every scriptural means to enlighten them with the gospel ? Are we a holy people ? Is our example such as our neighbours may follow ? Do we endeavour, even in meat and drink, to do all to the glory of God? Are we prayerful? Oh, the many churches that give up their prayer-meetings, because prayer is not in them! How can they expect a blessing? Are we united? Oh, brothers, it is a horrible thing when church members talk against one another, and even slander one another, as though they were enemies rather than friends. Can God bless such a church as that ? Let us search through and through the camp, lest there be an Achan, whose stolen wedge and Babylonian garment, hidden in his tent, shall bind the hands of the Almighty so that he cannot fight for his people. Let every church see to itself in this.

Next I speak to *Christian people* who have fallen into trouble through serving God. I put it to them, but I want to ask them a few questions. Are you quite sure that you did serve God in it ? You know there are men who indulge crotchets, and whims, and fancies. God has not promised to support you in your whims. Certain people are obstinate, and will not submit to what everybody must bear who has to earn his bread in a world like this. If you are a mere mule, and get the stick, I must leave you to your reward; but I speak to men of understanding. Be as stern as a Puritan against everything that is wrong, but be supple and yieldable to everything that involves self-denial on your part. God will bear us through if the quarrel be his quarrel ; but if it is our own quarrel, why then we may help ourselves. There is a deal of difference between being pig-headed and being steadfast. To be steadfast, as a matter of principle in truth which is taught by God's Word, is one thing ; but to get a queer idea into your heads is quite another.

Besides, some men are conscientious about certain things, but they have not an all-round conscience. Some are conscientious about not taking less, but they are not conscientious about giving less. Certain folks are conscientious about resting on the Sabbath ; but the other half of the command is, " Six days shalt thou labour," and they do not remember that portion of the law. I like a conscience which works fairly and impartially : but if your conscience gives way for the sake of your own gain or pleasure, the world will think that it is a sham, and they will not be far from the mark. But if, through conscientiousness, you should be a sufferer, God will bear you through. Only examine and see that your conscience is enlightened by the Spirit of God.

And now to conclude. I want to address *the seeking sinner.* Some are longing to find peace, but they cannot reach it ; and I want them to see whether they have not been negligent in some points so that they would not be able to say with Elijah, " I have done all these things at thy word."

Do I need to say that you cannot be saved by your works ? Do I need to repeat it over and over again that nothing you do can deserve mercy? Salvation must be the free gift of God. But this is the point. God will give pardon to a sinner, and peace to a troubled heart, on certain lines. Are you on those lines wholly ? If so, you will have peace ; and if you have not that peace, something or other has been omitted. To begin with, the first thing is *faith.* Dost thou believe that Jesus Christ is the Son of God ? Dost thou believe that he has risen from the dead ? Dost thou trust thyself wholly, simply, heartily, once for all, with him ? Then it is written,—" He that believeth in him hath everlasting life." Go and plead that. " I have no peace," says one. Hast thou unfeignedly *repented* of sin ? Is thy mind totally changed about sin, so that what thou didst once love thou dost now hate, and that which thou didst once hate thou dost now love ? Is there a hearty loathing, and giving up, and forsaking of sin ? Do not deceive yourself. You cannot be saved *in* your sins ; you are to be saved *from* your sins. You and your sins must part, or else Christ and you will never be joined. See to this. Labour to give up every sin, and turn from every false way, else your faith is but a dead faith, and will never save you. It may be that you have wronged a person, and have never made *restitution.* Mr. Moody did great good when he preached restitution. If we have wronged another we ought to make it up to him. We ought to return what we have stolen, if that be our sin. A man cannot expect peace of conscience till, as far as in him lies, he has made amends for any wrong he has done to his fellow-men. See to that, or else perhaps this stone may lie at your door, and because it is not rolled away you may never enter into peace.

It may be, my friend, that you have neglected *prayer.* Now, prayer is one of those things without which no man can find the Lord. This is how we seek him, and if we do not seek him how shall we find him ? If you have been neglectful in this matter of prayer, you cannot say, " I have done all these things at thy word." May the Lord stir you up to pray mightily, and not to let him go except he bless you ! In waiting upon the Lord he will cause you to find rest to your soul.

Possibly, however, you may be a believer in Christ, and you may have no peace because you are associated with ungodly people, and go with them to their follies, and mix with them in their amusements. You see you cannot serve God and Mammon. Thus saith the Lord, "Come out from among them : *be ye separate :* touch not the unclean thing, and I will be a Father unto you, and ye shall be my sons and daughters, saith the Lord Almighty." I know a man who sits in this place : he is probably here to-night : and concerning him I am persuaded that the only thing that keeps him from Christ is the company with which he mingles. I will not say that his company is bad in itself, but it is bad to him ; and if there be anything that is right in itself, yet if to me it becomes ruinous, I must give it up. We are not commanded to cut off warts and excrescences, but Jesus bids us cut off right arms, and pluck out right eyes—good things in themselves,—if they are stumbling-blocks in our way so that we cannot get at Christ. What is there in the world that is worth the keeping if it involves me in the loss of my soul ? Away with it. Hence many things which are lawful to another man, perhaps, to you may not be expedient because they are injurious. Many things cause no harm to the bulk of men, and yet to some one man they would be the most perilous things, and therefore he should avoid them. Be a law to yourselves, and keep clear of everything that keeps you away from the Saviour.

Perhaps, however, you say, " Well, as far as I know, I do keep out of all ill associations, and I am trying to follow the Lord." Let me press you with a home-question,—*will you be obedient to Jesus in everything ?*

> " For know—nor of the terms complain—
> Where Jesus comes he comes to reign."

If you would have Christ for a Saviour, you must also take him for a King. Therefore it is that he puts it to you " He that believeth and is baptized shall be saved." Will the baptism save me ? Assuredly not, for you have no right to be baptized until you are saved by faith in Jesus Christ ; but remember, if Christ gives you the command—if you accept him as a King—you are bound to obey him. If instead of saying " Be baptized " he had simply said, " Put a feather in your cap," you might have asked, " Will putting a feather in my cap save me ? " No, but you are bound to do it because he bids you. If he had said, " Put a stone in your pocket, and carry it with you " ; if that were Christ's command, it would be needful that you take the stone, and carry it with you. The less there seems to be of importance about a command, often the more hinges upon it. I have seen a rebellious boy, to whom his father has said, " Sir, pick up that stick. Pick up that stick." There is no very great importance about the command, and so the youth sullenly refuses to obey. " Do you hear, sir ? Pick up that stick." No : he will not. Now, if it had been a great thing that he had been bidden to do, which was somewhat beyond his power, it would not have been so clear an evidence of his rebellion when he refused to do it, as it is when it is but a little and trifling thing, and yet he refuses to obey. Therefore, I lay great stress upon this—that you who do believe in Jesus Christ should do according to his word. Say, " Lord, what wouldest thou have me to do ? Be it what it may, I will do it, for I am thy servant." I want you, if you would be Christ's, to be just like the brave men that rode at Balaclava.

> " Yours not to reason why ;
> Yours but to do and die "—

if it need be, if Jesus calls you thereto. Be this your song—

> " Through floods and flames if Jesus lead,
> I'll follow where he goes."

That kind of faith which at the very outset cries, " I shall not do that, it is not essential"; and then goes on to say, " I do not agree with that, and I do not agree with the other"; is no faith at all. In that case it is you that is master, and not Christ. In his own house you are beginning to alter his commands. " Oh," says one, " but as to baptism: I was baptized, you know, a great many years ago, when I was an infant." Say you so ? You have heard of Mary when her mistress said, " Mary, go into the drawing-room, and sweep it and dust it." Her mistress went into the drawing-room, and found it dusty. She said, " Mary, did you not sweep the room, and dust it ? " " Well, ma'am, yes I did : only I dusted it first, and then I swept it." That was the wrong order, and spoiled the whole ; and it will never do to put Christ's commands the other way upwards, because then they mean just nothing. We ought to do what he bids us, as he bids us, when he bids us, in the order in which he bids us. It is ours simply to be obedient, and when we are so, we may remember that to believe Christ and to obey Christ is the same thing, and often in Scripture the same word that might be read " believe," might be read " obey." He is the Author of eternal salvation to all them that obey him, and that is to all them that believe on him. Trust him then right heartily, and obey him right gladly. You can then go to him in the dying hour, and say, " Lord, I have done all these things at thy word. I claim no merit, but I do claim that thou keep thy gracious promise to me, for thou canst not run back from one word which thou hast spoken."

God bless you, beloved, for Christ's sake.

PORTION OF SCRIPTURE READ BEFORE SERMON—1 Kings xviii. 17—40.

HYMNS FROM "OUR OWN HYMN BOOK"—417, 515, 514.

Love's Law and Life

"If ye love me, keep my commandments."—John xiv. 15.

THIS is a chapter singularly full of certainties, and remarkably studded with *ifs*. Concerning most of the great things in it there never can be an " if "; and yet " if " comes up, I think, no less than seven times in the chapter; and " if," too, not about trifles, but about the most solemn subjects. It is, perhaps, worthy of mention that with each of these " ifs " there is something connected, as following out of it, or appearing to be involved in it, or connected with it.

Look at the second verse. " In my Father's house are many mansions : *if* it were not so, I would have told you." If there had been no place for us in the glory land Jesus would have told us. If any truth which had not been revealed would have made our hope a folly, our Lord Jesus would have warned us of it; for he has not come to lure us into a fool's paradise, and at last deceive us. He will tell us all that it is necessary for us to know in order to a wise faith and a sure hope. The Lord has not spoken in secret, in a dark place of the earth : he has not spoken in contradiction of his revealed word. Nothing in his secret decrees or hidden designs can shake our confidence, or darken our expectation. " *If* it were not so, I would have told you." Had there been a secret thing which would have injured your prospects, it should have been dragged to light, that you might not be deceived; for the Lord Jesus has no desire to win disciples by the suppression of distasteful truth. If there were anything yet to be revealed which would render your hope a delusion at the end, you should have been made acquainted with it; Jesus himself would break the sad news to you; he would not leave you to be horrified by finding it out for yourselves; he kindly declares, " I would have told you."

Notice the third verse. Again we meet with " if," and its consequence. " *If* I go and prepare a place for you, I will come again, and receive you unto myself." If the Lord Jesus should go away (and this is a supposition no longer, for he has gone), then he would return again in due time. Since he has gone, he will come again; for he has made the one to depend on the other. We make no question that he went up into heaven, for he rose from out the circle of his followers, and they saw him as he went up into heaven. They had no sort of doubt as to the fact that the cloud received him out of their sight; and, moreover, they received assurance out of heaven, by an angelic messenger, that "He shall so come in like manner as ye have seen him go into heaven." "If I go and prepare a place for you, I will come again, and receive you unto myself." His home-going pledges him to come, and compels us to look for him.

The next "if" comes at *the beginning of the seventh verse: "If* ye had known me, ye should have known my Father also." If we really do know the Lord Christ, we know God. In fact, there is no knowing God aright except through his Son Jesus. It is evidently true that men do not long hold to theism pure and simple. If our scientific men get away from the Christ, the incarnate God, before long they drift away from God altogether. They begin to slide down the mountain when they quit the incarnate Deity, and there is no more foothold to stay them. No man comes to the Father but by the Son, and no man long keeps to the Father who does not keep to his faith in the Son. Those who know Christ know God; but those who are ignorant of the Saviour are ignorant of God, however much they may pride themselves upon their religion. They may know another God, but the only living and true God is unknown save by those who receive Jesus. The divine Fatherhood, of which we hear so much in certain quarters, is only to be seen through the window of incarnation and sacrifice. We must see Jesus before we can gain even so much as a glimpse at the Infinite, the Incomprehensible, and the Invisible. God comes not within finite perception till he enters human flesh; and there we behold his glory, full of grace and truth.

The next variety of "if" you will find a little farther down in the chapter, namely, *in the fourteenth verse*: "*If* ye shall ask any thing in my name, I will do it." The "if" in this case involves an uncertainty about our prayers, if an uncertainty at all. Taking it for granted that we ask mercies in the name of Jesus, a glorious certainty is linked thereto. Jesus saith, "I will do it." Here our Lord speaks after a sovereign style. *We* may not say, "I will"; but the "I wills" pertain to Christ. He can answer, and he has the right to answer, and therefore he says without reservation, "I will." "If ye shall ask anything in my name, I will do it." Oh that we might put the first "if" out of court by continually petitioning the Lord, and signing our petitions with the name of Jesus! May we be importunate only in prayers to which we are warranted to set that august name; and then boldly using his name and authority, we need be under no apprehension of failure. The great Father in heaven never denies the power of his Son's name, neither does the Son himself draw back from the keeping of his own pledges. True prayer operates with the same certainty as the laws of nature. "Delight thyself also in the Lord; and he shall give thee the desires of thine heart." Oh that we did delight more in the Divine name and character, and then our prayers would always speed at the throne!

Now comes the "if" of our text, of which I will say nothing for the moment. "If ye love me, keep my commandments." Something, you see, is to come out of this "if" as out of all the others. *If* something, *then* something—" *If* ye love me," then carry it out to the legitimate result : "keep my commandments."

You have the next "if" in verse 23 : "Jesus answered and said unto him, *If* a man love me, he will keep my words." Respect to his wisdom, and obedience to his authority, will grow out of love. "The love of Christ constraineth us." We hear that passage often quoted, "The love of Christ ought to constrain us"; but that is a corruption of the text : the apostle tells us that it does constrain us ; and if it really enters the heart, it will do so. It is an active, moving power, influencing the inner life, and then the external conduct.

> " 'Tis love that makes our willing feet
> In swift obedience move."

"If a man love me, he will keep my words." He will believe in the verbal inspiration of his Lord ; he will regard his teaching as infallible ; he will attend to it and remember it. More than this, he will by his conduct carry out the words of his Lord, and so keep them in the best possible manner by enshrining them in his daily life.

The chapter almost closes at the twenty-eighth verse by saying, "If ye loved me, ye would rejoice, because I said, I go unto my Father ; for my Father is greater than I." Where there is an intelligent love to Christ we rejoice in his gains even though we ourselves appear to be losers thereby. The corporeal absence of our Lord from our midst might seem to be a great loss to us ; but we rejoice in it because it is for his own greater glory. If he is enthroned in glory, we dare not lament his absence. Our love agrees to his departure, yea, rejoices in it ; for anything which conduces to his exaltation is sweet to us. Let us at this moment, because we love him, rejoice that he has gone to the Father.

So you see the chapter, if you read it, though enriched with heavenl, certainties, is yet besprinkled with "ifs." Like little pools of sparkling water among the ever abiding rocks, these "ifs" gleam in the light of heaven, and refresh us even to look upon them.

Let us now think of our own text, and may the Holy Spirit lead us into the secret chambers of it! "*If* ye love me, keep my commandments."

The present "if" is a serious one. Let that stand as our first head. Secondly, *the test which is added concerning it is a very judicious one :* "If ye love me, keep my commandments." In the third place, I will give you the reading of the Revised Version, and say, *that test will be endured by love ;* for the words may be interpreted—"If ye love me, ye will keep my commandments." Obedience will follow upon love as a matter of certainty.

I. To begin, then, THE IF IN OUR TEXT IS A VERY SERIOUS ONE. It goes to the very root of the matter. Love belongs to the heart ; and every surgeon will tell you that a disease of the heart may not be trifled with. A clever doctor said to me, "I feel at my ease with any matter if it does not touch the head or the heart." Solomon bids us keep the heart with all diligence, "for out of it are the issues of life." If the mainspring fails, all the works of a watch refuse to act. We cannot, therefore, think little of a question which concerns our love, for it deals with a vital part. O friends, I hope there is no question about our love to Jesus.

Observe how our Saviour puts this *if* concerning love, in such a way as to teach us that *love must be prior to obedience*. The text is not, "Keep my commandments, and then love me." No, we do not expect pure streams till the fountain is cleansed. Nor does he say—"Keep my commandments, and love me at the same time," as two separate things, although that might in a measure correspond with truth. But love is put first, because it is first in importance and first in experience. "If ye love me"—we must begin with love: then "keep my commandments." Obedience must have love for its mother, nurse, and food. The essence of obedience lies in the hearty love which prompts the deed rather than in the deed itself. I can conceive it possible that a man might, in his outward life, keep Christ's commandments, and yet might never keep them at all so as to be accepted before God. If he became obedient by compulsion, but would have disobeyed if he dared, then his heart was not right before God, and his actions were of little worth. The commandments are to be kept out of love to him who gave them. In obedience, to love is to live: if we love Christ we live Christ. Love to the person of our Lord is the very salt of our sacrifices. To put it most practically—I often say to myself, "To-day I have performed all the duties of my office; but have I been careful to abide in my Lord's love? I have not failed as to doing all that was possible to me; I have gone from early morning till late at night, packing as much work as possible into every hour, and trying to do it with all my heart. But have I, after all, done this as unto the Lord and for his sake?" I tremble lest I should serve God merely because I happen to be a minister and am called to preach his word; or because the natural routine of the day carries me through it. I am concerned that I may be impelled by no force but the love of Jesus. This fear often humbles me in the dust, and prevents all glorying in what I have done. Only as we love our Lord can our obedience be true and acceptable. The main care of our lives should be to do right, and to do it because we love the Lord. We must walk before the Lord as Abraham did, and with the Lord as Enoch did. Unless we are under the constant constraint of love to the Lord Jesus Christ we shall fail terribly.

> "Knowledge, alas! is all in vain,
> And all in vain our fear,
> In vain our labour and our pain
> If love be absent there."

See, dear friends, how inward true religion is : how far it exceeds all external formalism! How deep is the seat of true grace! You cannot hope to do that which Christ can smile upon until your heart is renewed. A heart at enmity with God cannot be made acceptable by mere acts of piety. It is not what your hands are doing, nor even what your lips are saying; the main thing is what your heart is meaning and intending. Which way are your affections tending? The great fly-wheel which moves the whole machinery of life is fixed in the heart : hence this is the most important of all suggestions—"If ye love me." "If ye love me" is a searching sound. I start as I hear it. He that believes in the Lord Jesus Christ for his salvation produces as the first fruit of his faith love to Christ; this must be in us and abound, or nothing is right. Packed away within that box of sweets called "love" you shall find every holy thing; but if you have no love, what have you? Though you wear your fingers to the bone with service, weep out your eyes with repentance, make your knees hard with kneeling, and dry your throat with shouting, yet if the heart does not beat with love your religion falls to the ground like a withered leaf in autumn. Love is the chief jewel in the bracelet of obedience. Hear the text, and mark it well: "If ye love me, keep my commandments."

O sirs, what a mass of religion is cast out as worthless by this text! Men may keep on going to church and going to chapel, and they may be religious, ay, throughout a whole life; and, apparently, they may be blameless in their moral conduct, and yet there may be nothing in them, because there is no love to the ever-blessed Christ at the bottom of the profession. When the heathen killed their sacrifices in order to prophesy future events from the entrails, the worst augury they ever got was when the priest, after searching into the victim, could not find a heart; or if that heart was small and shrivelled. The soothsayers always declared that this omen was the sure sign of calamity. All the signs were evil if the heart of the offering was absent or deficient. It is so in very deed with religion and with each religious person. He that searches us searches principally our hearts. He who tries mankind tries chiefly the reins of the children of men. The Master is in our midst to-night, walking down these aisles with noiseless tread, girt about the paps with a golden girdle, and robed in snow-white garments down to his feet. See, he stops before each one of us, and gently asks, "Lovest thou me?" Three times he repeats the question. He waits for an answer. It is a vital question: do not refuse a reply. Oh that the Spirit of the Lord may enable you to answer in sincerity and truth, and say, "Lord, thou knowest all things; thou knowest that I love thee"!

This matter of love to Jesus is put prior to every other because *it is the best reason for our obedience to him.* Notice: "If ye love *me*, keep *my* commandments." Personal affection will produce personal obedience. Do you not see the drift of the words? The blessed Jesus says, "If you love *me*, keep *my* commandments"; because, truly, operative love is mainly love to a person, and love to our Lord's person begets obedience to his precepts. There are some men for whom you would do anything: you will to yield to their will. If such a person were to say to you, "Do this," you would do it without question. Perhaps he stands to you in the relation of master, and you are his willing servant. Perhaps he is a venerated friend, and because you esteem and love him, his word is law to you. The Saviour may much more safely than any other be installed in such a position. From the throne of your affections he says, "If ye love me—if really your hearts go out to me—then let my word be a commandment; let my commandment be kept in your memory, and then further kept by being observed in your life. So you see the reason why the Master begins with the heart—because there is no hope of obedience to him in our actions, unless he is enshrined in our affections. This is the spring and source of all holy living—love to the Holy One. Dear friends, have you been captured by the beauties of Jesus, and are you held in a divine captivity to the adorable person of your redeeming Lord? Then you have within you the impulse which constrains you to keep his commandments.

It was greatly needful for our Lord thus to address his disciples. Yes, it was necessary to speak thus even to the apostles. He says to the chosen twelve, "If ye love me." We should never have doubted one of them. We now know by the result that one of them was a traitor to his Lord, and sold him for pieces of silver; but no one suspected him, for he seemed as loyal as any one of them. Ah! if that question, "If ye love me," needed to be raised in the sacred college of the twelve, much more must it be allowed to sift our churches, and to test ourselves. Brethren, this word is exceedingly needful, in the present assembly : hear its voice—"If ye love me." The mixed multitude here gathered together may be compared to the heap on the threshing-floor, and there is need of the winnowing fan. Perhaps you have almost taken it for granted that you love Jesus ; but it must not be taken for granted. Some of you have been born in a religious atmosphere, you have lived in the midst of godly people, and you have never been out into the wicked world to be tempted by its follies ; therefore you come to an immediate conclusion that you must assuredly love the Lord. This is unwise and perilous. Never glory in armour which you have not tested, nor rejoice in love to Christ which has not sustained trial. What an awful thing if you should be deceived and mistaken ! It is most kind of the Saviour to raise a question about your love, and thus give you an opportunity of examining yourself and seeing whether you are right at heart. It will be far better for you to err upon the side of too great anxiety than on that of carnal security. To be afraid that you are wrong, and so to make sure of being right, will bring you to a far better end than being sure that you are right, and, therefore, refusing to look into the ground of your hope. I would have you fully assured of your love to Jesus, but I would not have you deceived by a belief that you love him if you do not. Lord, search us and try us !

Remember, if any man love not the Lord Jesus Christ he will be *anathema maranatha,* cursed at his coming. This applies to every man, even though he be most eminent. An apostle turned out to be a son of perdition—may not you? Every man, even though he be a learned bishop, or a popular pastor, or a renowned evangelist, or a venerable elder, or an active deacon, or the most ancient member of the most orthodox assembly, may yet turn out to be no lover of the Lord. Though he has gathered to break bread in the sacred name with a select company, yet if he doth not truly love the Lord Jesus Christ, the curse rests upon him, whoever he may me. So let us take from the Master's lip the heart-searching word at this time, "If ye love me, keep my commandments." Let us take it personally home, as if addressed to each one of us personally and alone.

While considering the text, let each one view himself apart. What have you to do in this matter with keeping the vineyards of others? See to your own hearts. The text does not say, "If the church loves me," **or,** " If such and such a minister loves me," or, " If your brothers love me"; but it is, " If *ye* love me, keep my commandments." The most important question for each one to answer is that which concerns his personal attachment to his Redeemer, and the personal obedience which comes out of it. I press this enquiry upon each one. It may seem a trite and commonplace question, but it needs to be put again and again before all in our congregations. The preacher needs to be thus questioned: he gets into the habit of reading his Bible for other people. The Sunday-school teacher needs this enquiry: he also is apt to study the Scriptures rather for his class than for himself. We all need the truth to come home to us with personal and forcible application, for we are always inclined to shift unpleasant enquiries upon others. In the case of very deaf people, when they hold up their horns we speak right down into them; and I wish to speak home pointedly to each one of you at this time. Let the text sound into your individual ear and heart: " If ye love me, keep my commandments."

The question is answerable, however. It was put to the apostles, and they could answer it. Peter spoke as all the eleven would have done when he said, " Thou knowest that I love thee." It is not a question concerning mysteries out of range and beyond judgment: it deals with a plain matter of fact. A man may know whether he loves the Lord or not, and he ought to know. He who is jealous of himself, and is, therefore, half afraid to speak positively, may all the more truly be a lover of the Lord. Holy caution may raise a question where the answer is far more certain than in the breasts of those who never even make the enquiry, because they are carnally secure. Do not be content with merely longing to love Jesus; or with longing to know whether you love him. Not to know whether you love the Lord Jesus is a state of mind so dangerous that I exhort you never to go to sleep till you have escaped from it. A man has no right to smile—I had almost said, he has no right either to eat bread or drink water so long as that question hangs in the balances. It ought to be decided. It can be decided. It can be decided at once. Not love Jesus? It were better for me not to live than not to love *him.* Not love Christ? May the terrible fact never be hidden from my weeping eyes! Perhaps the dread discovery may drive me to better things. If I do love my Lord I can never rest with the shadow of a doubt darkening the life of my love. A question on such a matter is unbearable.

> " Do not I love thee from my soul?
>   Then let me nothing love :
> Dead be my heart to every joy,
>   When Jesus cannot move.

> " Would not my heart pour forth its blood
>   In honour of thy name,
> And challenge the cold hand of death
>   To damp the immortal flame?

> " Thou know'st I love thee, dearest Lord;
>   But oh, I long to soar
> Far from the sphere of mortal joys,
>   And learn to love thee more."

Brethren, hear the question suggested by this little word "*if*"; consider it well, and rest not until you can say, "I love the Lord because he hath heard my voice and my supplication."

So much, then, concerning the serious nature of this *if*.

II. In the second place, let me observe that THE TEST WHICH IS PROPOSED IN THE TEXT IS A VERY JUDICIOUS ONE. "If ye love me, *keep my commandments.*" This is the best proof of love.

The test indicated does not suggest a lawless liberty. It is true we are not under the law, but under grace ; but yet we are under law to Christ, and if we love him we are to keep his commandments. Let us never enter into the counsel of those who do not believe that there are any commandments for believers to keep. Those who do away with duty do away with sin, and consequently with the Saviour. It is not written —If ye love me, do whatever you please. Jesus does not say—so long as you love me in your hearts, I care nothing about your lives. There is no such doctrine as that between the covers of this holy book. He that loves Christ is the freest man out of heaven, but he is also the most under bonds. He is free, for Christ has loosed his bonds, but he is put under bonds to Christ by grateful love. The love of Christ constraineth him henceforth to live to the Lord who loved him, lived for him, died for him, and rose again. No, dear friends, we do not desire a lawless life. He that is not under the law as a power for condemnation, yet can say that with his heart he delights in the law of God; he longs after perfect holiness, and in his soul yields hearty homage to the precepts of the Lord Jesus. Love is law : the law of love is the strongest of all laws. Christ has become our Master and King, and his commandments are not grievous.

The text also contains no fanatical challenge. We do not read, "If ye love me, perform some extraordinary act." The test required is not an outburst of extravagance, or an attempt to realize the ambitious project of a fevered brain. Nothing of the kind. Hermits, nuns, and religious mad-caps find no example or precept here. Some persons think that if they love Jesus, they must enter a convent, retire to a cell, dress themselves queerly, or shave their heads. It has been the thought of some men, "If we love Christ we must strip ourselves of everything we possess, put on sackcloth, tie ropes round our waists, and pine in the desert." Others have thought it wise to make guys of themselves by oddity of dress and behaviour. The Saviour does not say anything of the kind ; but, "If ye love me, keep my commandments." Every now and then we find members of our churches who must needs leave their trades and their callings to show their love for Jesus : children may starve and wives may pine, but their mad whimsies must be carried out for love of Jesus. Under this influence they rush into all sorts of foolery, and soon ruin their characters because they will not take the advice of sobriety, and cannot be satisfied with the grand test of love which our Lord himself herein lays down. The text does not condemn these light-headed projects in detail, but it does so in the gross by proposing a far more reasonable test—"If ye love me, keep my commandments." Do not spin theories in your excited brains, and vow that you will do this desperate thing and the other. The probability is that you are not seeking the glory of the Lord, but you are wanting notoriety for yourself. You are aiming at supreme devotion, that you may become a distinguished person, and that people may talk about your superior saintship. You may even go so far as to court persecution from selfish motives. The Saviour, who was wise and knew what was in men, and knew also what would be the surest test of true love to himself, says, " If ye love me, *keep my commandments.*" This is a much more difficult thing than to follow out the dictates of a crazy brain.

Why does the Saviour give us this as a test? I think that one reason is, because it is one which *tests whether you are loving Christ in his true position,* or whether your love is to a Christ of your own making, and your own placing. It is easy to crave a half Christ, and refuse a whole Christ. It is easy also to follow a Christ of your own construction, who is merely an antichrist. The real Christ is so great and glorious that he has a right to give commandments. Moses never used an expression such as our Saviour here employs. He might say, " Keep God's commandments"; but he would never have said, " Keep *my* commandments." That dear and Divine Person whom we call Master and Lord here says, " Keep *my* commandments." What a commanding person he must be! What lordship he has over his people! How great he is among his saints! If you keep his commandments you are putting him into the position which he claims. By obedience you own his sovereignty and Godhead, and say with Thomas, " My Lord and my God." I am afraid that a great many people know a Christ who is meek and lowly, their servant and Saviour; but they do not know the *Lord* Jesus Christ. Alas! my friends, such people set up a false Christ. We do not love Jesus at all if he is not our Lord and God. It is all cant and hypocrisy, this love to Christ which robs him of his Deity. I abhor that love to Christ which does not make him King of kings, and Lord of lords. Love him, and belittle him! It is absurd. Follow your own will in preference to his will, and then talk of love to him! Ridiculous! This is but the devil's counterfeit of love: it is a contradiction of all true love. Love is loyal: love crowns its Lord with obedience. If you love Jesus aright, you view his every precept as a divine commandment. You love the true Christ if you love a commanding Christ as well as a saving Christ, and look to him for the guidance of your life as well as for the pardon of your sin.

This test, again, is very judicious, because *it proves the living presence of the object of your love.* Love always desires to have its object near, and it has a faculty of bringing its object near. If you love anybody, that person may be far away, and yet to your thoughts he is close at hand. Love brings the beloved one so near that the thought of him acts upon its life. A gentleman has faithful servants; he goes away, and leaves his house in their charge: he has gone abroad, and yet he is at home to his servants, for every day their work is done as if he were there to see. He is coming home soon; they hardly know when, but they keep all things in readiness for his return, let it happen when it may. They are not eye-servants, and so they work none the less because he is absent. If he does not see *them,* yet the eyes of their love always see *him,* and therefore they work as if he were at home. Their affection keeps him ever near. A dear father is dead, and he has left his property to a son who honours his memory. What does the son do? He is generous, like his father; and when he is asked why, he replies, " I do exactly what I believe my dear father would have done if he had been here." " Why?" "Because I love him." When a man is dead he lives to those who love him? So the living Christ, who is not dead, but has gone away, is made present to us by our realizing love; and the proof of our love is that Jesus is so present that he constrains our actions, influences our motives, and is the cause of our obedience. Jesus seems to say—" If you love me, now that I am gone you will do as you would have done if I were still with you, and looking at you. You will continue to keep my commandments, as in my presence."

It is a most judicious test, again, because, by keeping our Lord's commandments, *we are doing that which is most pleasing to him, and will most glorify him.* Some enthusiastic Methodist cries—

" Oh, what shall I do my Saviour to praise?"

Hearken, my brother: if you love your Saviour, keep his commandments. This is all you have to do, and a great all too. Among the rest, you may come and be baptized, while you are thus earnest to praise your Lord. " If ye love me, keep my commandments." There is the answer to every rapturous enquiry. Jesus is more glorified by a consistent obedience to his commands than by the most extravagant zeal that we can possibly display in what is only will-worship, because he has never commanded it. If you wish to break the alabaster box, and fill the house with sweet perfume; if you wish to crown his head with rarest gems; the method is before you—" Keep my commandments." You cannot do your Lord so great a favour, or, in the long run, bring to him so real an honour, as by a complete, continual, hearty obedience to every one of his commandments.

Moreover, the Saviour knew, when he bade us try this test, " If ye love me, keep my commandments," that *it would prepare us for honouring and glorifying him in any other ways.* Read the context: " If ye love me, keep my commandments. And I will pray the Father, and he shall give you another Comforter, that he may abide with you for ever." You can greatly glorify Christ if you are filled with the Holy Spirit; but you cannot be filled with the Holy Spirit if you do not keep Christ's commandments. The Spirit of God as a Comforter will come only to those to whom he comes as a Sanctifier. By making us holy, he will qualify us for being useful. The Saviour says, " If ye love me, keep my commandments," because we shall then obtain that divine gift by which we can glorify his name. If there be any service which your love would aspire to, obedience to your Lord is the way to it.

But, indeed, I need not stand here and argue. When a friend is dying, and he asks you to prove your love by such and such a deed, he may ask what he wills; you give him *carte blanche.* It may be the simplest thing or the hardest thing; but if he will prescribe it as a test of love, you will not say him nay. If your wife should say to you, " You are going to journey far from me, and I shall not see you again for many days; I beg you therefore to carry my portrait within your watch-case," you would not fail to do so. It would be a simple thing, but it would be sacred to you. Baptism and the Lord's Supper will never be slighted by those whose hearts are fully possessed with love to Jesus. They may seem trifles, but if the Lord Jesus commands them they cannot be neglected. To leave off your wedding-ring might be no great crime; and yet no loving wife would do it: even so, none who regard outward ordinances as love-tokens will think of neglecting them. Ours not to ask for reasons, ours not to dispute about whether the deed is essential or non-essential; ours to obey right lovingly. Bridegroom of our hearts, say what thou wilt, and we will obey thee! If only thou wilt smile and strengthen us, nothing shall be impossible if great, nothing trifling if small.

III. Time has wellnigh gone, or we would dwell upon the third head, which we must now leave, only praying God to prove the truth of it. The third head was this: TRUE LOVE WILL ENDURE THIS TEST. "If ye love me, ye will keep my commandments." This is the Revised Version, and I hope it will be written out in capitals upon our revised lives! We will obey, we must obey, since we love him by whom the command is given.

Come then, brothers and sisters, as the time has gone, let me say this much to you. If you love Christ, set to work to *find out what his commandments are.* Study the Scriptures upon every point upon which you have the slightest question. This sacred oracle must guide you.

Next, *be always true to your convictions* about what Christ's commandments are. Carry them out at all hazards, and carry them out at once. It will be wicked to say, "Hitherto I have obeyed, but I shall stop here." We are committed to implicit obedience to the whole of the Master's will, involve what it may. Will you not agree to this at the outset? If you love him, you will not demur.

Take note of every commandment as it concerns you. Let me mention one or two, and beg you to obey them as you hear them. "Go ye into all the world, and preach the gospel to every creature." Is not this a call to you, my brother, to be a missionary? Do you hear it? Will you not say, "Here am I; send me"? Another person has come into this house to-night full of enmity: somebody has treated him very badly, and he cannot forget it; I pray him to hear the Lord's command: "Therefore if thou bring thy gift to the altar, and there rememberest that thy brother hath ought against thee; leave there thy gift before the altar, and go thy way; first be reconciled to thy brother, and then come and offer thy gift." And again: "Little children, love one another." If any of you are in debt, obey this commandment: "Owe no man anything, but to love one another." If you neglect the poor, and live in a niggardly way, hear this commandment: "Give to him that asketh thee, and from him that would borrow of thee turn not thou away." At the back of all comes this, "If ye love me, keep my commandments." I might stop here all night, and mention, one after another, the commandments which would be specially applicable to each one of my hearers; but I pray the Holy Ghost to bring all things to your remembrance.

If there be a commandment which you do not relish, it ought to be a warning to you that there is something wrong in your heart that needs setting right. If ever you quarrel with one of Christ's commands, end that quarrel by specially attending to it beyond every other.

Do as the miserly man did when he conquered his avarice once for all. He was a Christian, and he promised he would give a pound to the church ; but the devil whispered, "You want your money ; do not pay." The man stamped his foot, and said, "I will give two." Then the devil said, "Surely you are going mad. Save your money." The man replied that he would not be conquered, he would give four pounds. "Now," said Satan, "You must be insane." Then said the man, "I will give eight ; and if you don't stop your tempting, I will give sixteen, for I will not be the slave of covetousness." The point is to throw your whole soul into that very duty wherein you are most tempted to be slack. Jesus does not say, if ye love me, keep this commandment or that, but out of love obey every command.

Many of you do not love my Lord Jesus Christ. I have not preached to you, but that very fact should make you thoughtful. Go home and consider that the preacher said nothing to you because you do not love the Lord Jesus Christ, and therefore cannot keep his commandments. Write down in black and white—" *I do not love the Lord Jesus Christ.*" If it be really so, be honest enough to make a note of it, and think it over. If you love Jesus, you may joyfully write out, " I love the Lord Jesus. Oh for grace to love him more!" But if you do not love him it will be honest to put it upon record. Write it boldly : " *I do not love the Lord Jesus Christ.*" Look at it, and look again ; and oh, may God the Holy Ghost lead you to repent of not loving Jesus, who is the altogether lovely One, and the great lover of men's souls! Oh that you may begin to love him at once ! Amen and Amen.

PORTION OF SCRIPTURE READ BEFORE SERMON—John xiv.

HYMNS FROM " OUR OWN HYMN BOOK "—792, 809, 654.

The Man Who Shall Never See Death*

" Verily, verily, I say unto you, If a man keep my saying, he shall never see death. Then said the Jews unto him, Now we know that thou hast a devil. Abraham is dead, and the prophets; and thou sayest, If a man keep my saying, he shall never taste of death. Art thou greater than our father Abraham, which is dead? and the prophets are dead: whom makest thou thyself? "—John viii. 51—53.

IN the previous part of this chapter we hear the Jews, with malicious voices, assailing our blessed Lord with this bitter question, " Say we not well that thou art a Samaritan, and hast a devil? " How very quietly the Saviour answered them! He did answer them, because he judged it needful to do so; but he did so with great patience, and with sound argument: " I have not a devil; but I honour my Father." Clear proof this! No man can be said to have a devil who honours God; for the evil spirit from the beginning has been the enemy of all that glorifies the Father. Paul, who had not read this passage—for the Gospel of John was not then written—was nevertheless so filled with his Master's spirit, that he answered after a like manner when Festus said, " Paul, thou art beside thyself; much learning doth make thee mad." He calmly replied, " I am not mad, most noble Festus; but speak forth the words of truth and soberness." This was a fine copy of our Saviour's gentle and forcible reply : " I have not a devil; but I honour my Father." Brethren, whenever you are falsely accused, and an evil name is hurled at you, if you must needs reply, " give a reason of the hope that is in you with meekness and fear." Be not heated and hurried; for if so, you will lose strength, and will be apt to err. Let your Lord be your model.

---

* This sermon was preached, in great sorrow, after the sudden death of the senior deacon of the Tabernacle church, Mr. WILLIAM OLNEY. He had been more than fifty years a member, and for many years our right-hand man. His zeal in service was only rivalled by his patience in suffering. Love was his prominent characteristic. He was graciously impetuous, and yet persistently constant. While he was a very ready speaker, he was not a mere talker ; but was as liberal with his gifts, and as abundant in his prayers, as he was frequent in his exhortations. Never Pastor had abler or more earnest helper. His son right worthily sustains the honour of the house; but scarcely could any dozen workers fill up the gap which the father's death has caused in the departments of prayer-meetings, foreign missions, home evangelization, and orphanage. Help, Lord, for a great man hath fallen in our Israel !—C. H. S.

The false charge was the occasion of our Lord's uttering a great truth. On they rush, furious in their rage, but he flashes in their faces the light of truth. To put down error, lift up truth. Thus their deadly saying was met by a living saying: "Verily, verily, I say unto you, If a man keep my saying, he shall never see death." Nothing so baffles the adversaries of the faith as to utter with unshaken confidence the truth of God. The truth which Jesus stated was full of promise; and if they wilfully rejected his promise, it became worse to them than a threatening. Christ's rejected promises curdle into woes. If these men, when he said to them, "If a man keep my saying he shall never see death," yet went on reviling him, then their consciences, when afterwards awakened, would say to them, "He that believeth not shall not see life; but the wrath of God abideth on him." If the believer shall never see death, then the unbeliever shall never see life. Thus the gospel itself becomes "a savour of death unto death" to those who refuse it; and the very word which proclaims eternal life threatens eternal death to the wilfully unbelieving. I pray that, this morning, we may be put into a gracious frame of mind, and may be so helped to keep Christ's saying, that we may inherit this wondrous promise: "If a man keep my saying, he shall never see death."

May the Holy Spirit specially aid me while I first speak upon *the gracious character*: the man who keeps Christ's saying. Secondly, I would dwell upon *the glorious deliverance*: "He shall never see death." Thirdly, taking the two later verses of my text, I would honour *the great Quickener;* for evidently, according to the Jews, our Lord was making much of himself by what he said; and in truth the fact that the believer shall never see death does greatly magnify the Lord Jesus. May he be glorified in our mourning hearts while we think of our departed friend as one who shall never see death!

I. First, consider THE GRACIOUS CHARACTER: "If a man keep my saying, he shall never see death."

Observe, that *the one conspicuous characteristic of the man who shall never behold death is that he keeps Christ's saying or word.* He may have other characteristics, but they are comparatively unimportant in this respect. He may be of a timorous nature; he may often be in distress; but if he keep Christ's saying, he shall never see death. He may have been a great sinner in his early life; but, being converted, and led to keep Christ's saying, he shall never see death. He may be a strong-minded man, who keeps a firm grip of eternal realities, and therefore becomes supremely useful; but none the more for that is this promise true to him: the reason for his safety is the same as in the case of the weak and timorous: he keeps Christ's saying, and therefore he shall never see death. Divest yourselves, therefore, of all enquiries about other matters, and only make inquisition in your own heart upon this one point: do you keep Christ's saying? If you do this, you shall never see death.

Who is this man who keeps Christ's saying? Obviously, *he is a man that has close dealing with Christ.* He hears what he says; he notes what he says; he clings to what he says. We meet with persons nowadays who talk about faith in God; but they know not the Lord

Jesus Christ as the great sacrifice and reconciler. But without a mediator there is no coming to God. Jesus says, "No man cometh unto the Father, but by me." His witness is true. Brethren, we glorify Christ as himself God. Truly, the unity of the Godhead is never doubted among us; but while "there is one God," there is also "one mediator between God and man, the man Christ Jesus." For ever remember that Christ Jesus as God-man, Mediator, is essential to all our intercourse with the Father. You cannot trust God, nor love God, nor serve God aright, unless you willingly consent to his appointed way of reconciliation, redemption, justification, and access, which is only through the precious blood of Jesus Christ. In Christ we draw nigh unto God. Attempt not to approach unto Jehovah, who is a consuming fire, except through the incarnate God. Tell me, my hearer, is your faith fixed upon him whom God has set forth to be the propitiation for sin? Do you come to God in God's own way? for he will not receive you in any other. If you reject the way of salvation through the blood of the Lamb, you cannot be keeping the saying of Christ; for he says, "He that hath seen me hath seen the Father"; and he says this of none else.

These people, next, making the Lord Jesus their all in all, reverenced his word, and therefore kept it: they respected, observed, trusted, and obeyed it. By keeping his saying is meant, first, that *they accept his doctrine.* Whatever he has laid down as truth is truth to them. My hearer, is it so with you? With some their great source of belief is their own thought. They judge the divine revelation itself, and claim the right, not only to interpret it, but to correct and expand it. In the fulness of self-confidence, they make themselves the judges of God's Word. They believe a doctrine because the light of the present age confirms it or invents it. Their foundation is in man's own thought. In their opinion, parts of Scripture are exceedingly faulty, and need tinkering with scientific hammers. The light of the Holy Ghost is to them a mere glowworm as compared with the light of the present advanced age. But he that is to share the promise now before us is one who believes the Saviour's word, because it *is* his word. He takes the sayings of Christ, and his inspired apostles, as being therefore true, because so spoken. To him the inspiration of the Holy Ghost is the warrant of faith. A very important matter this: the foundation of our faith is even more important than the superstructure. Unless you ground your faith upon the fact that the Lord hath spoken, your faith lacks that worshipful reverence which God requires. Even if you are correct in your beliefs, you are not correct in your spirit unless your faith is grounded on the authority of God's own Word. We are to be disciples, not critics. We have done with cavilling, for we have come to believing. In this our departed deacon stood on firm ground. By him every teaching of the Word was accepted with a lively, childlike faith; and though tempted by the school of doubt, he was not in the least affected by its reasonings. To him the gospel was dear as life itself. As *he* did, so must we believe Christ's doctrines.

Next, the gracious man *trusts Christ's promises.* This is a crucial point. Without trust in Jesus we have no spiritual life. Say, my hearer, dost thou rely upon the saying of the Lord Jesus, "He that believeth in me hath everlasting life"? Dost thou believe in the promise of pardon to the man that confesseth and forsaketh his sin—pardon through the precious blood of the great sacrifice? Are the promises of Christ certainties to thee, certainties hall-marked with his sacred "Verily, verily, I say unto you"? Canst thou hang thy soul upon the sure nail of the Lord's saying? Some of us rest our eternal destiny solely upon the truthfulness of Christ. When we take all his promises together, what a fulness of confidence they create in us!

> "How firm a foundation, ye saints of the Lord,
> Is laid for your faith in his excellent word!"

Furthermore, the gracious man *obeys his precepts*. No man can be said to keep Christ's saying unless he follows it practically in his life. He is not only teacher, but Lord to us. A true keeper of the Word cultivates that spirit of love which is the very essence of Christ's moral teaching. He endeavours to be meek and merciful. He aims at purity of heart, and peaceableness of spirit. He follows after holiness even at the cost of persecution. Whatsoever he finds that his Lord has ordained, he cheerfully performs. He does not kick at the Lord's command, as involving too much self-denial and separation from the world; but he is willing to enter in by the strait gate, and to follow the narrow way, because his Lord commands him. That faith which does not lead to obedience is a dead faith and a false faith. That faith which does not cause us to forsake sin, is no better than the faith of devils, even if it be so good.

> "Faith must obey her Father's will,
> As well as trust his grace:
> A pardoning God is jealous still
> For his own holiness."

So, now you see who the man is that keeps Christ's saying. That man receives, through the Word of God, a new and everlasting life; for the Word of God is a "living and incorruptible seed, which liveth and abideth for ever." Wherever the seed of the Word drops into a soil which accepts it, it takes root, abides and grows. "For God so loved the world, that he gave his only-begotten Son, that whosoever believeth in him should not perish, but have everlasting life." It is by Christ's saying, or by Christ's Word, that life is implanted in the soul: by that same word the heavenly life is fed, increased, developed, and at length perfected. The power and energy of the Holy Ghost which work through the word are used as the beginning, the sustaining, and the perfecting of the inner life. The life of grace on earth is the blossom of which the life of glory is the fruit. It is the same life all along, from regeneration to resurrection. The life which comes into the soul of the believer, when he begins to keep Christ's sayings, is the same life which he will enjoy before the eternal throne in the realms of the blessed.

We may know what keeping Christ's saying is from the fact that he himself has set us the example. Note well the fifty-fifth verse, where Jesus says concerning the Father—"Yet ye have not known him; but I know him: and if I should say, I know him not, I shall be a liar like unto you: but *I know him, and keep his saying.*" We are to keep our Lord's saying, even as he kept his Father's saying. He lived upon the Father's word, and therefore refused Satan's temptation to turn stones into bread. His Father's word was in him, so that he always did the things which pleased the Father. When he spoke, he spoke not his own words, but the word of him that sent him. He lived that the divine word might be executed: even on the cross he was careful that the Scripture might be fulfilled. He said, "He that is of God heareth God's words"; and this was so truly the case with him that he said, "Mine ears hast thou opened." The word was everything to him, and he rejoiced over his apostles, because he could say of them, "They have kept thy word." He, whose word you are to keep shows you how to keep it. Live towards him as he lived towards the Father, and then you shall receive the promise he has made: "Verily, verily, I say unto you, If a man keep my saying, he shall never see death." If love be the fulfilling of the Lord's saying, our dearly-beloved but now departed friend kept the saying of Christ—for in that matter many believers have done virtuously, but he excelled them all. He has not looked on death.

II. Now we turn to the delightful part of our subject, namely, THE GLORIOUS DELIVERANCE which our Lord here promises: "He shall never see death." Our Lord did not mean that he shall never die, for he died himself; and his followers, in long procession, have descended to the grave. Some brethren are cheered by the belief that they shall live until the Lord comes, and therefore they shall not sleep, but shall only be changed. The hope of our Lord's appearing is a very blessed one, come when he may; but I do not conceive that to be alive at his coming is any great object of desire. Is there any great preference in being changed beyond that of dying? Do we not read that, "We which are alive and remain unto the coming of the Lord shall not prevent them which are asleep"? This is a great truth. Throughout eternity, if I die I shall be able to say I had actual fellowship with Christ in the article of death, and in descent into the grave, which those happy saints who will survive can never know. It is no matter of doctrine, but yet, if one might have a choice in the matter, it might be gain to die.

> "The graves of all his saints he bless'd,
> And soften'd every bed :
> Where should the dying members rest,
> But with the dying Head?"

How dear will Christ be to us when, in the ages to come, we shall think of his death, and shall be able to say, "We, too, have died and risen again"! You that are alive and remain will certainly not have a preference over us, who, like our Lord, shall taste of death. I am only speaking now of a matter of no great moment, which, as believers, we may use as a pleasant subject of discourse among ourselves. We grieve not that our brother has fallen asleep before the Lord's glorious appearing, for we are sure that he will be no loser thereby. Our Lord has said, "If a man keep my saying, he shall never see death"; and this does not relate to the few who will remain at his second advent, but to the entire company of those who have kept his saying, even though they pass into the grave.

What does this promise mean? It means this, in the first place: *our face is turned away from death.* Here am I, a poor sinner, convinced of sin, and aroused to a fear of wrath. What is there before my face? What am I compelled to gaze upon? The Greek is not fully interpreted by the word " see ": it is an intenser word. According to Westcott, the sight here mentioned is that of "a long, steady, exhaustive vision, whereby we become slowly acquainted with the nature of the object to which it is directed." The awakened sinner is made to look at eternal death, which is the threatened punishment of sin. He stands gazing upon the result of sin with terror and dismay. Oh, the wrath to come! The death that never dies! While unforgiven, I cannot help gazing upon it, and foreseeing it as my doom. When the gospel of the Lord Jesus comes to my soul, and I keep his saying by faith, I am turned completely round. My back is upon death, and my face is towards life eternal. Death is removed; life is received; and more life is promised. What do I see within, around, and before me? Why, life, and only life—life in Christ Jesus. " He is our life." In my future course on earth, what do I see? Final falling from grace? By no means; for Jesus saith, "I give unto my sheep eternal life." What do I see far away in the eternities? Unending life. " He that believeth in me hath everlasting life." Now I begin to realize the meaning of that text, " I am the resurrection: he that believeth in me, though he were dead, yet shall he live." And again, " I am the life: he that liveth and believeth in me shall never die." The man who has received the saying of the Lord Jesus has passed from death unto life, and shall never come into condemnation, and consequently shall never gaze on death. All that lies before the believer is life, life more abundantly, life to the full, life eternal. What has become of our death? Our Lord endured it. He died for us. " He his own self bare our sins in his own body on the tree." In his death as our representative we died. There is no death penalty left for the believer; for not the least charge can be brought against those for whom Christ has died. Hence we sing—

> " Complete atonement thou hast made,
>   And to the utmost farthing paid
>   Whate'er thy people owed:
>   Nor can his wrath on me take place,
>   If shelter'd in thy righteousness,
>   And sprinkled with thy blood."

Shall *we* die for whom Christ died in the purpose of God? Can our departure out of the world be sent as a punishment, when our Lord Jesus has so vindicated justice that no punishment is required? When I behold my Lord die upon the cross, I see that for me death itself is dead.

Then comes in another sense of the expression. " He that keepeth my saying shall never see death," means that *his spiritual death is gone never to return.* Before the man knows Christ, he abideth in death,

and wherever he looks he sees nothing but death. Poor souls! *you* know what I am talking about, *you* that are now under concern of soul; for you try to pray, and find death in your prayers; you try to believe, but seem dead as to faith. Alas, you ungodly ones! although you know it not, death is everywhere within you. You are "dead in trespasses and sins." Your sins are to you what grave-clothes are to a corpse; they seem your natural investiture; they cling to you, they bind you. Little do you know what corruption is coming upon you, so that God himself will say of you, "Bury the dead out of my sight." As soon as ever the gospel saying of the Lord Jesus comes to a man with power, what is the effect? He is dead no longer: he begins to see life. It may be, that at first it is a painful life—a life of deep regrets for the past, and dark fears for the future; a life of hungering and thirsting; a life of pining and panting; a life that wants a something, it scarcely knows what, but it cannot live without it. This man sees life; and the more he keeps his Saviour's word, the more he rejoices in Christ Jesus, the more he rests on his promise, the more he loves him, the more he serves him, the more will his new life drive death out of sight. Life now abounds and holds sway, and the old death hides away in holes and corners. Though oftentimes the believer has to mourn over the old death which struggles to return, yet he does not gaze upon that death of sin as once he did; he cannot endure it, he takes no pleasure in the contemplation of it, but cries to God for deliverance from it. Grace frees us from the reign of death as well as from the penalty of death; and in neither of these senses shall the keeper of Christ's saying ever look upon death.

"But," cries one, "will not a Christian man die?" I answer, not necessarily; for some will remain at the coming of our Lord, and these will not die; and hence there is no legal necessity that any should die, since the obligation would then rest alike on all. But good men die. The tokens of death are seen in mournful array upon my pulpit. Yet our dear brother did not die as the penalty of his sin. He was forgiven; and it is not according to God's grace or justice to punish those whom he has forgiven. O my hearers, if you do not believe in the Lord Jesus, death will be a penal infliction *to you;* but death is changed in its nature in the case of a believer in Jesus. Our death is a falling asleep, not a going to execution. It is a departure out of the world unto the Father, not a being driven away in wrath. We quit the militant host of earth for the triumphant armies of heaven by the gate of death; that which was a cavern leading to blackness and darkness for ever, has, by the resurrection of our Lord, been made into an open tunnel, which serves as a passage into eternal glory. As a penal infliction upon believers, death was abolished by our Lord; and now it has become a stairway from the grace-life below to the glory-life above.

"If a man keep my saying, he shall never gaze on death," may further mean, *he shall not live under the influence of it.* He shall not be perpetually thinking of death and dreading its approach, and that which follows after it. I must admit that some Christians are in bondage through fear of death; but that is because they do not keep their Master's saying as they ought to do. The effect of his saying upon us is frequently such that instead of being afraid to die, we come to long to depart. In such a case we should realize the verses of Watts, who tells us that could we see the saints above, we should long to join them.

> " How we should scorn these robes of flesh,
> These fetters and this load !
> And long for evening to undress,
> That we may rest in God.
>
> " We should almost forsake our clay
> Before the summons come,
> And pray and wish our souls away
> To their eternal home."

I have to check some dear brethren when they say to me, " Let me die the death of the righteous." No, do not talk as Balaam did ; but rather say, "Let me live, that I may glorify God and help my sorrowing brethren in the Lord's work." I pray you, do not hasten to be gone ; and yet this impatience proves that death has lost its terrors for us. We do not see death looming before us as a coming tempest : we do not gaze upon it as a fascinating horror which makes our faces pale, and casts a lurid glare on all around. We see not the darkness, for we walk in the light : we fear not the rumbling of the chariot, for we know who rides to us therein.

We shall never see that which is the reality and essence of death, namely, the wrath of God in the second death. We have no cause to fear condemnation, for " it is God that justifieth." That final separation from God, which is the real death of human nature, can never come to us. " Who shall separate us from the love of God, which is in Christ Jesus our Lord ! " That ruin and misery which the word " death " describes, when used in relation to the soul, will never befall us ; for we shall never perish, neither shall any pluck us out of Christ's hand.

When the believer dies, he does not gaze on death. He walks through the valley of the shadow of death ; but he fears no evil, and sees none to fear. A shadow was cast across my road, but I passed through it, and scarcely perceived that it was there. Why was that ? Because I had my eye fixed upon a strong light beyond ; and I did not notice the shadow which otherwise would have distressed me. Believers are so rejoiced by the presence of their Lord and Master, that they do not observe that they are dying. They rest so sweetly in the embrace of Jesus, that they hear not the voice of wailing. When they pass from one world into another, it is something like going from England to Scotland : it is all one kingdom, and one sun shines in both lands. Often travellers by railway ask, " When do we pass from England into Scotland ? " There is no jerk in the movement of the train ; no broad boundary : you glide from one into the other, and scarce know where the boundary lies. The eternal life that is in the believer glides along from grace to glory without a break We grow steadily on from the blade to the ear, and from the ear to the full corn ; but no black belt divides the stages of growth from one another. We shall know when we arrive; but the passage may be so rapid that we shall not see it. From earth to heaven may

seem the greatest of journeys, but it is ended in the twinkling of an **eye.**

> " One gentle sigh, the fetter breaks,
> We scarce can say, ' He's gone,'
> Before the ransomed spirit takes
> Its mansion near the throne."

He shall never gaze on death : he shall pass it by with no more than a glance. He shall go through Jordan as though it were dry land, and scarce know that he has passed a river at all. Like Peter, the departing shall scarce be sure that they have passed through the iron gate, which shall open of its own accord ; they shall only know that they are free. Of each one of them it may be said, as of Peter, " He wist not that it was true which was done by the angel ; but thought he saw a vision." Fear not death; for Jesus says, " He that keepeth my saying shall never see death."

Follow the soul when it enters upon the other world : the body is left behind, and the man is a disembodied spirit; but he does not see death. All the life he needs he has within his soul by being one with Jesus. Meanwhile, he is expecting that at the trump of the resurrection his body will be reunited with his soul, having been made to be the dwelling and the instrument of his perfected spirit. While he is absent from the body, he is so present with the Lord that he does not look on death.

But the judgment-day has come, the great white throne is set, the multitudes appear before the Judge? What about the keeper of Christ's saying? Is he not afraid? It is the day of days, the day of wrath! He knows that he shall never see death, and therefore he is in no confusion. For him there is no " Depart, ye cursed." He can never come under the eternal sentence. See! hell opens wide her mouth tremendous. The pit which of old was digged for the wicked yawns and receives them. Down sink the ungodly multitude, a very cataract of souls. " The wicked shall be turned into hell, and all the nations that forget God." In that terrific hour, will not his foot slip ? No; he shall stand in the judgment, and shall never see death.

But the world is in a blaze ; all things are being dissolved, and the elements are melting with fervent heat ; the stars are falling like the leaves of autumn, and the sun is black as sackcloth of hair. Is he not now alarmed? Ah, no ! He shall never see death. His eyes are fixed on life, and he himself is full of it. He abides in life, he spends that life in praising God. He shall never gaze on death ; for Jesus says, " Because I live, ye shall live also." O blessed eyes, that shall never look on death ! O happy mind, that has been made confident in Jesus Christ of an immortality for which there is no hazard ! Our dear brother was the embodiment of life in the service of the Lord. Last Sabbath he sat in this seat behind me, and responded in his very soul to the Word of the Lord. Last Monday was spent all day in the service of God and this church, in the most hearty manner. Though a great sufferer, his spirit carried him over his bodily weakness, and he constantly exhibited an amazing zeal for God and the souls of men. To the last the old ruling passion was strong in him : he would speak for his Lord. He was so struck down that he did not know that he was dying. He found himself in heaven or ever he was aware, and I dare say he said to himself, "I thought I was going to the Tabernacle; but here I am in the temple of my God. For many a year I took my seat among my brethren below, or went about serving my Lord among his people, and now I have a mansion above, and behold his face; but I will now see what there is to do." Yes, he will serve God day and night in his temple, just as he did here; for he was never tired of work for Jesus. He was always at it, and always full of life. He never beheld death while he was with us, for he overflowed with life; and when physical death came, he did not gaze upon it, but simply bowed his head, and found himself before the throne.

What a glorious word is this! Alas for you who are ungodly! you are made to look on death. It haunts you now; what will it be in the hour of your decease? "What will you do in the swelling of Jordan?" Nothing remains for you but the wages of sin, which is death. The ruin and misery of your souls will be your endless portion. You will be shut in with the finally destroyed, ruined, and wretched ones for ever! This is a dreadful looking for of judgment. It ought to startle you. But as for the believer, surely the bitterness of death is past. We have nothing more to do with death as a penalty or a terror, any more than we have to do with spiritual death as the choke-damp of the heart, and the mother of corruption.

III. This brings me to the third point—THE GREAT QUICKENER. Those Jews—what a passion they were in! How unscrupulous their talk! They could not even quote Christ's words correctly. They said, "Thou sayest, If a man keep my saying, he shall never *taste* of death." He did not say so. He said, "Shall never *see* death." We may be said to taste of death as our Master did; for it is written that "He tasted death for every man." And yet in another sense we shall never taste the wormwood and gall of death, for to us it is "swallowed up in victory." Its drop of gall is lost in the bowl of victory. However, the Lord Jesus did not say that we shall never taste of death; neither did he mean that we shall not die, in the common sense of the word. He was using, to the Jews, words in that religious sense in which their own prophets used them. The ancient Scriptures so used the word death; and these Jews knew their meaning right well. Death did not always mean the separation of the soul from the body; for the Lord's declaration to Adam was, "In the day that thou eatest thereof thou shalt surely die." Assuredly, Adam and Eve died in the sense intended; but they were not annihilated, nor were their souls separated from their bodies; for they still remained to labour on earth. "The soul that sinneth it shall die," relates to a death which consists of degradation, misery, inability, ruin. Death does not mean annihilation, but something very different. Overthrow and ruin are the death of a soul, just as perfection and joy are its life for ever. The separation of the soul from God is the death penalty; and that is death indeed. The Jews refused to understand our Lord; yet they clearly saw that what Jesus claimed tended to glorify him above Abraham and the prophets. Hidden away in their abusive words, we find a sense which is instructive. It is not the greatness or the goodness of a believer that secures his eternal life; *it is his being linked by faith to the Lord Jesus Christ,* who is greater than Abraham and the prophets. The man keeps Christ's saying, and that becomes a bond between him and Christ, and he is one with Christ. Because of their Lord, the saints live; and the living of the saints by him brings to him glory and honour. His life is seen in every one of his people: like mirrors, they reflect his divine life. He has life in himself, and that life he imparts to his chosen. As the old creation displays the glory of the Father, so the new creation reveals the glory of the Son. Believers find their highest life in Christ Jesus their Lord, and every particle of it glorifies him.

It is also to our Lord's glory that we live by his word. He does not sustain us by the machinery of providence, but by his word. As the world stood out into being because God spake, so do we live and continue to live because of Christ's saying. That which he taught, being received into our hearts, becomes the origin and the nourishment of our eternal life. It is greatly glorifying to Christ that, by his word, all spiritual life in the countless myriads of believers is begotten and sustained.

It is clear that the Lord Jesus is far greater than Abraham and all the prophets. Their word could not make men live, nor even live themselves. But the saying of Jesus makes all live who receive it. By keeping it they live—yea, live for ever. Glory be to the name of him who quickeneth whom he wills!

A sweet inference flows from all this, and with that I conclude. *The glory of Christ depends upon the not seeing of death by all who keep his saying.* If you and I keep his saying, and we see death, then Jesus is not true. If you, believing in Jesus, gaze on death, it will be proved that either he had not the power or the will to make his promise good. If the Lord fails in any one case, he has lost the honour of his faithfulness. O ye trembling, anxious souls, lay hold on this:

> " His honour is engaged to save
> The meanest of his sheep."

If the saint of God, who has won thousands for Jesus, should after all perish, what a failure of covenant engagements there would be! But that failure would be just as great if one of the least of all those who keep our Lord's word should be suffered to perish. Such a loss of honour to our all-glorious Lord is not to be imagined; and hence if one of you who are the least in your father's house do really trust in him, though encumbered with infirmities and imperfections, he must keep you from beholding death. His truth, his power, his immutability, his love, are all involved in his faithfulness to his promise to each believer. I want you to take this home with you, and be comforted.

Ay, and if I have some foul transgressor here this morning, the grossest sinner that ever lived, if thou wilt come to Christ, lay hold upon his gracious saying, keep it, and be obedient to it, thou shalt never see death. There is not a soul in hell that can ever say, "I have kept Christ's saying, and I have seen death, for here I am." There never will be one such, or Christ's glory would be tarnished throughout eternity. Keep his saying, and he will keep you from seeing death!

How eagerly did my departed friend long for the conversion of those who came to the Tabernacle! He was never satisfied while any were unblessed. He had great longings. He loved revivals and missions. Tidings of souls saved stirred his inmost soul. Oh, that his prayers, while he was with us, may be answered now that he is gone from us! He not only lived among us, but he lived in our hearts. He needs no praise from me; his praise is in all the church. He will require no monument; all your hearts are his memorials. Never can I forget my beloved fellow-worker either in time or in eternity. Beloved, the real William Olney has not seen death, although with many tears we must lay him in the grave next Wednesday. Pray much for me: my loss is not to be measured. Pray much for his dear family, whose loss cannot be repaired. Amen.

PORTION OF SCRIPTURE READ BEFORE SERMON—Revelation vii.

HYMNS FROM "OUR OWN HYMN BOOK"—875, 877, 872.

The Obedience of Faith

"By faith Abraham, when he was called to go out into a place which he should after receive for an inheritance, obeyed; and he went out, not knowing whither he went."—Hebrews xi. 8.

THE part of the text to which I shall call your attention lies in these words, "*By faith Abraham obeyed.*" Obedience—what a blessing it would be if we were all trained to it by the Holy Spirit! How fully should we be restored if we were perfect in it! If all the world would obey the Lord, what a heaven on earth there would be! Perfect obedience to God would mean love among men, justice to all classes, and peace in every land. Our will brings envy, malice, war; but the Lord's will would bring us love, joy, rest, bliss. Obedience—let us pray for it for ourselves and others!

> "Is there a heart that will not bend
> To thy divine control?
> Descend, O sovereign love, descend,
> And melt that stubborn soul!"

Surely, though we have had to mourn our disobedience with many tears and sighs, we now find joy in yielding ourselves as servants of the Lord: our deepest desire is to do the Lord's will in all things. Oh, for obedience! It has been supposed by many ill-instructed people that the doctrine of justification by faith is opposed to the teaching of good works, or obedience. There is no truth in the supposition. We preach the obedience of faith. Faith is the fountain, the foundation, and the fosterer of obedience. Men obey not God till they believe him. We preach faith in order that men may be brought to obedience. To disbelieve is to disobey. One of the first signs of practical obedience is found in the obedience of the mind, the understanding, and the heart; and this is expressed in believing the teaching of Christ, trusting to his work, and resting in his salvation. Faith is the morning star of obedience. If we would work the work of God, we must believe on Jesus Christ whom he hath sent. Brethren, we do not give a secondary place to obedience, as some suppose. We look upon the obedience of the heart to the will of God as salvation. The attainment of perfect obedience would mean perfect salvation. We regard sanctification, or obedience, as the great design for which the Saviour died. He shed his blood that he might cleanse us from dead works, and purify unto himself a people zealous for good works. It is for this that we were chosen: we are "elect unto holiness." We know nothing of election to continue in sin. It is for this that we have been called: we are "called to be saints." Obedience is the grand object of the work of grace in the hearts of those who are chosen and called: they are to become obedient children, conformed to the image of the Elder Brother, with whom the Father is well pleased.

The obedience that comes of faith is of a noble sort. The obedience of a slave ranks very little higher than the obedience of a well-trained horse or dog, for it is tuned to the crack of the whip. Obedience which is not cheerfully rendered is not the obedience of the heart, and consequently is of little worth before God. If the man obeys because he has no opportunity of doing otherwise, and if, were he free, he would at once become a rebel—there is nothing in his obedience. The obedience of faith springs from a principle within, and not from compulsion without. It is sustained by the mind's soberest reasoning, and the heart's warmest passion. The man reasons with himself that he ought to obey his Redeemer, his Father, his God; and, at the same time, the love of Christ constrains him so to do, and thus what argument suggests affection performs. A sense of great obligation, an apprehension of the fitness of obedience, and spiritual renewal of heart, work an obedience which becomes essential to the sanctified soul. Hence, it is not relaxed in the time of temptation, nor destroyed in the hour of losses and sufferings. Life has no trial which can turn the gracious soul from its passion for obedience; and death itself doth but enable it to render an obedience which shall be as blissful as it will be complete. Yes, this is a chief ingredient of heaven—that we shall see the face of our Lord, and serve him day and night in his temple. Meanwhile, the more fully we obey at this present, the nearer we shall be to his temple-gate. May the Holy Spirit work in us, so that, by faith—like Abraham—we may obey!

I preach to you, at this time, obedience—absolute obedience to the Lord God; but I preach the obedience of a child, not the obedience of a slave; the obedience of love, not of terror; the obedience of faith, not of dread. I shall urge you, as God shall help me, in order that you may come at this obedience, that you should seek after stronger faith—"For by faith Abraham obeyed." In every case where the father of the faithful obeyed, it was the result of his faith; and in every case in which you and I shall render true obedience, it will be the product of our faith. Obedience, such as God can accept, never cometh out of a heart which thinks God a liar; but is wrought in us by the Spirit of the Lord, through our believing in the truth, and love, and grace of our God in Christ Jesus. If any of you are now disobedient, or have been so, the road to a better state of things is trust in God. You cannot hope to render obedience by the mere forcing of conduct into a certain groove, or by a personal, unaided effort of the resolution. There is a free-grace road to obedience, and that is receiving, by faith, the Lord Jesus, who is the gift of God, and is made of God unto us sanctification. We accept the Lord Jesus by faith, and he teaches us obedience, and creates it in us. The more of faith in him you have, the more of obedience to him will you manifest. I was about to say that that obedience naturally flows out of faith, and I should not have spoken amiss, for as a man believeth so is he, and in proportion to the strength and purity of his faith in God, as he is revealed in Christ Jesus, will be the holy obedience of his life.

That our meditation may be profitable, we will first think a little of *the kind of faith which produces obedience;* and then, secondly, we will treat of *the kind of obedience which faith produces;* and then we will advance another step, and consider *the kind of life which comes out of this faith and obedience.*

I will be as brief as I can upon each point. Let us look up to the Holy Ghost for his gracious illumination.

I. First, consider THE KIND OF FAITH WHICH PRODUCES OBEDIENCE. It is, manifestly, *faith in God as having the right to command our obedience.* Beloved in the Lord, you know that he is Sovereign, and that his will is law. You feel that God, your Maker, your Preserver, your Redeemer, and your Father, should have your unswerving service. We unite, also, in confessing that we are not our own, we are bought with a price. The Lord our God has a right to us which we would not wish to question. He has a greater claim upon our ardent service than he has upon the services of angels; for, while they were created as we have been, yet they have never been redeemed by precious blood. Our glorious Incarnate God has an unquestioned right to every breath we breathe, to every thought we think, to every moment of our lives, and to every capacity of our being. We believe in Jehovah as rightful Lawgiver, and as most fitly our Ruler. This loyalty of our mind is based on faith, and is a chief prompter to obedience. Cultivate always this feeling. The Lord is our Father, but he is, "our Father which art in heaven." He draws near to us in condescension; but it is condescension, and we must not presume to think of him as though he were such a one as ourselves. There is a holy familiarity with God which cannot be too much enjoyed; but there is a flippant familiarity with God which cannot be too much abhorred. The Lord is King; his will is not to be questioned; his every word is law. Let us never question his sovereign right to decree what he pleases, and to fulfil the decree; to command what he pleases, and to punish every shortcoming. Because we have faith in God as Lord of all, we gladly pay him our homage, and desire in all things to say: "Thy will be done in earth, as it is done in heaven."

Next, we must have *faith in the rightness of all that God says or does.* I hope, beloved, you do not think of God's sovereignty as tyranny, or imagine that he ever could or would will anything but that which is right. Neither will we admit into our minds a suspicion of the incorrectness of the Word of God in any matter whatever, as though the Lord himself could err. We will not have it that God, in his Holy Book, makes mistakes about matters of history, or of science, any more than he does upon the great truths of salvation. If the Lord be God, he must be infallible; and if he can be described as in error in the little respects of human history and science, he cannot be trusted in the greater matters. My brethren, Jehovah never errs in deed, or in word; and when you find his law written either in the ten commandments, or anywhere else, you believe that there is not a precept too many, or too few. Whatever may be the precepts of the law, or of the gospel, they are pure and holy altogether. The words of the Lord are like fine gold, pure, precious, and weighty—not one of them may be neglected. We hear people talk about "minor points," and so on; but we must not consider any word of our God as a minor thing, if by that expression is implied that it is of small importance. We must accept every single word of precept, or prohibition, or instruction, as being what it ought to be, and neither to be diminished nor increased. We should not reason about the command of God as though it might be set aside or amended. He bids: we obey. May we enter into that true spirit of obedience which is the unshaken belief that the Lord is right! Nothing short of this is the obedience of the inner man—the obedience which the Lord desires.

Furthermore, we must have *faith in the Lord's call upon us to obey*. Abraham went out from his father's house because he felt that, whatever God said to others, he had spoken to him, and said, "Get thee out of thy country, and from thy kindred, and from thy father's house." Whatever the Lord may have said to the Chaldæans, or to other families in Ur, Abraham was not so much concerned with that as with the special word of command which the Lord had sent to his own soul. Oh, that we were most of all earnest to render personal obedience! It is very easy to offer unto God a sort of "other people's obedience"—to fancy that we are serving God, when we are finding fault with our neighbours, and lamenting that they are not so godly as they ought to be. Truly, we cannot help seeing their shortcomings; but we should do well to be less observant of them than we are. Let us turn our magnifying glasses upon ourselves. It is not so much our business to be weeding other people's gardens as to keep our own vineyard. To the Lord each one should cry, "Lord, what wilt thou have *me* to do?" We, who are his chosen, redeemed from among men, called out from the rest of mankind, ought to feel that if no other ears hear the divine call, our ears must hear it; and if no other heart obeys, our soul rejoices to do so. We are bound with cords to the horns of the altar. The strongest ties of gratitude hold us to the service of Jesus: we must be obedient in life to him who, for our sakes, was obedient unto death. Our service to our Lord is freedom: we will to yield to his will. To delight him is our delight. It is a blessed thing when the inmost nature yearns to obey God, when obedience grows into a habit, and becomes the very element in which the spirit breathes. Surely it should be so with every one of the blood-washed children of the Most High, and their lives will prove that it is so. Others are bound to obey, but we should attend most to our own personal obligation, and set our own houses in order. Our obedience should begin at home, and it will find its hands full enough there.

Obedience arises out of a *faith which is to us the paramount principle of action*. The kind of faith which produces obedience is lord of the understanding, a royal faith. The true believer believes in God beyond all his belief in anything else, and everything else. He can say, "Let God be true, but every man a liar." His faith in God has become to him the crown of all his believings; the most assured of all his confidences. As gold is to the inferior metals, such is our trust in God to all our other trusts. To the genuine believer the eternal is as much above the temporal as the heavens are above the earth. The infinite rolls, like Noah's flood, over the tops of the hills of the present and the finite. To the believer, let a truth be tinctured with the glory of God, and he values it; but if God and eternity be not there, he will leave these trifles to those who choose them. You must have a paramount faith in God, or else the will of God will not be a paramount rule to you. Only a reigning faith will make us subject to its power, so as to be in all things obedient to the Lord. The chief thought in life with the true believer is, "How can I obey God?" His great anxiety is to do the will of God, or acceptably to suffer that will; and if he can obey, he will make no terms with God, and stand upon no reservations. He will pray, "Refine me from the dross of rebellion, and let the furnace be as fierce as thou wilt." His choice is neither wealth, nor ease, nor honour; but that he may glorify God in his body, and his spirit, which are the Lord's. Obedience has become as much his rule as self-will is the rule of others. His cry unto the Lord is, "By thy command I stay or go. Thy will is my will; thy pleasure is my pleasure; thy law is my love."

God grant us a supreme, over-mastering faith, for this is the kind of faith which we must have if we are to lead obedient lives! We must have faith in God's right to rule, faith in the rightness of his commands, faith in our personal obligation to obey, and faith that the command must be the paramount authority of our being. With this faith of God's elect, we shall realize the object of our election—namely, that we should be holy, and without blame before him in love.

Dear friend, have you this kind of faith? I will withdraw the question as directed to you, and I will ask it of myself: Have I that faith which leads me to obey my God?—for obedience, if it be of the kind we are speaking of, is faith in action—faith walking with God, or, shall I say, walking before the Lord in the land of the living? If we have a faith which is greedy in hearing, severe in judging, and rapid in self-congratulation, but not inclined to obedience, we have the faith of hypocrites. If our faith enables us to set up as patterns of sound doctrine, and qualifies us to crack the heads of all who differ from us, and yet lacks the fruit of obedience, it will leave us among the "dogs" who are "without." The faith that makes us obey is alone the faith which marks the children of God. It is better to have the faith that obeys than the faith which moves mountains. I would sooner have the faith which obeys than the faith which heaps the altar of God with sacrifices, and perfumes his courts with incense. I would rather obey God than rule an empire; for, after all, the loftiest sovereignty a soul can inherit is to have dominion over self by rendering believing obedience to the Most High.

Thus much upon faith. "By faith Abraham obeyed;" and by faith only can you and I obey.

II. Let us consider, secondly, THE KIND OF OBEDIENCE WHICH FAITH PRODUCES. This I shall illustrate from the whole of the verse.

Genuine faith in God creates a prompt obedience. "By faith Abraham, *when he was called,* obeyed." There was an immediate response to the command. Delayed obedience is disobedience. I wish some Christians, who put off duty, would remember this. Continued delay of duty is a continuous sin. If I do not obey the divine command, I sin; and every moment that I continue in that condition, I repeat the sin. This is a serious matter. If a certain act is my duty at this hour, and I leave it undone, I have sinned; but it will be equally incumbent upon me during the next hour; and if I still refuse, I disobey again, and so on till I do obey. Neglect of a standing command must grow very grievous if it be persisted in for years. In proportion as the conscience becomes callous upon the subject, the guilt becomes the more provoking to the Lord. To refuse to do right is a great evil; but to continue in that refusal till conscience grows numb upon the matter is far worse. I remember a person coming to be baptized, who said that he had been a believer in the Lord Jesus for forty years; and that he had always seen the ordinance to be Scriptural. I felt grieved that he had so long been disobedient to a known duty, and I proposed to him that he should be baptized at once. It was in a village, and he said that there were no conveniences. I offered to go with him to the brook, and baptize him, but he said, "No; he that believeth shall not make haste." Here was one who had wilfully disobeyed his Lord, for as many years as the Israelites in the wilderness, upon a matter so easy of performance; and yet, after confessing his fault, he was not willing to amend it, but perverted a passage of Scripture to excuse him in further delay. David says, "I made haste, and delayed not to keep thy commandments." I give this case as a typical illustration; there are a hundred spiritual, moral, domestic, business, and religious duties, which men put off in the same manner, as if they thought that any time would do for God, and he must take his turn with the rest. What would you say to your boy, if you bade him go upon an errand, and he answered you, "I will go to-morrow." Surely you would "morrow" him in a style which would abide upon his memory. Your tone would be sharp, and you would bid him go at once. If he, then, promised to run in an hour's time, would you call that obedience? It would be impudence. Obedience is for the present tense: it must be prompt, or it is nothing. Obedience respects the time of the command as much as any other part of it. To hesitate is to be disloyal. To halt and consider whether you will obey or not, is rebellion in the germ. If thou believest in the living God unto eternal life, thou wilt be quick to do thy Lord's bidding, even as a maid hearkens to her mistress. Thou wilt not be as the horse, which needs whip and spur; thy love will do more for thee than compulsion could do for slaves. Thou wilt have wings to thy heels to hasten thee along the way of obedience. "To-day, if ye will hear his voice, harden not your hearts."

Next, *obedience should be exact.* Even Abraham's obedience failed somewhat in this at first; for he started at once from Ur of the Chaldees, but he only went as far as Haran, and there he stayed till his father died; and then the precept came to him again, and he set off for the land which the Lord had promised to show him. If any of you have only half obeyed, I pray that you may take heed of this, and do all that the Lord commands, carefully endeavouring to keep back no part of the revenue of obedience.

Yet the error of the great patriarch was soon corrected, for we read that "Abraham, *when he was called to go out . . . went out.*" I have only omitted intermediate words, which do not alter the sense: and that is exactly how we should obey. That which the Lord commands we should do—just *that*, and not another thing of our own devising. How very curiously people try to give God something else instead of what he asks for! The Lord says, "My son, give me thine heart," and they give him ceremonies. He asks of them obedience, and they give him will-worship. He asks faith, and love, and justice; and they offer ten thousand rivers of oil, and the fat of fed beasts. They will give all except the one thing which he will be pleased with: yet "to obey is better than sacrifice, and to hearken than the fat of rams." If the Lord has given you true faith in himself, you will be anxious not so much to do a notable thing as to do exactly what God would have you to do. Mind your jots and tittles with the Lord's precepts. Attention to little things is a fine feature in obedience: it lies much more as to its essence in the little things than in the great ones. Few dare rush into great crimes, and yet they will indulge in secret rebellion, for their heart is not right with God. Hence so many mar what they call obedience by forgetting that they serve a heart-searching, rein-trying God, who observes thoughts and motives. He would have us obey him with the heart, and that will lead us, not merely to regard a few pleasing commands, but to have respect unto all his will. Oh, for a tender conscience, which will not wilfully neglect, nor presumptuously transgress!

And next, mark well that Abraham rendered *practical obedience.* When the Lord commanded Abraham to quit his father's house, he did not say that he would think it over; he did not discuss it *pro* and *con,* in an essay; he did not ask his father, Terah, and his neighbours to consider it; but, as he was called to go out, he went out. Alas! dear friends, we have so much talk, and so little obedience! The religion of mere brain and jaw does not amount to much. We want the religion of hands and feet. I remember a place in Yorkshire, years ago, where a good man said to me, " We have a real good minister." I said, "I am glad to hear it." "Yes," he said; "he is a fellow that preaches with his feet." Well, now, that is a capital thing if a preacher preaches with his feet by walking with God, and with his hands by working for God. He does well who glorifies God by where he goes, and by what he does; he will excel fifty others who only preach religion with their tongues. You, dear hearers, are not good hearers so long as you are only hearers; but when the heart is affected by the ear, and the hand follows the heart, then your faith is proved. That kind of obedience which comes of faith in God is real obedience, since it shows itself by its works.

Next, *faith produces a far-seeing obedience.* Note this. "Abraham, when he was called to go out into a place which he should *after* receive for an inheritance." How great a company would obey God if they were paid for it on the spot! They have "respect unto the recompense of the reward;" but they must have it in the palm of their hand. With them—"A bird in hand is better far, than two which in the bushes are." They are told that there is heaven to be had, and they answer that, if heaven were to be had here, as an immediate freehold, they might look after it, but they cannot afford to wait. To inherit a country after this life is over is too like a fairy tale for their practical minds. Many there are who enquire, "Will religion pay? Is there anything to be made out of it? Shall I have to shut up my shop on Sundays? Must I alter my mode of dealing, and curtail my profits?" When they have totalled up the cost, and have taken all things into consideration, they come to the conclusion that obedience to God is a luxury which they can dispense with, at least until near the end of life. Those who practise the obedience of faith look for the reward hereafter, and set the greatest store by it. To their faith alone the profit is exceeding great. To take up the cross will be to carry a burden, but it will also be to find rest. They know the words, "No cross, no crown;" and they recognize the truth that, if there is no obedience here, there will be no reward hereafter. This needs a faith that has eyes which can see afar off, across the black torrent of death, and within the veil which parts us from the unseen. A man will not obey God unless he has learned to endure "as seeing him who is invisible."

Yet, remember that *the obedience which comes of true faith is often bound to be altogether unreckoning and implicit;* for it is written, "He went out, not knowing whither he went." God bade Abraham journey, and he moved his camp at once. Into the unknown land he made his way; through fertile regions, or across a wilderness; among friends, or through the midst of foes, he pursued his journey. He did not know where his way would take him, but he knew that the Lord had bidden him go. Even bad men will obey God when they think fit; but good men will obey when they know not what to think of it. It is not ours to judge the Lord's command, but to follow it. I am weary with hearing men saying, "Yes, we know that such a course would be right; but then the consequences might be painful: good men would be grieved, the cause would be weakened, and we ourselves should get into a world of trouble, and put our hands into a hornet's nest." There is not much need to preach caution nowadays: those who would run any risk for the truth's sake are few enough. Consciences, tender about the Lord's honour, have not been produced for the last few years in any great number. Prudent consideration of consequences is superabundant; but the spirit which obeys, and dares all things for Christ's sake—where is it? The Abrahams of to-day will not go out from their kindred; they will put up with anything sooner than risk their livelihoods. If they do go out, they must know where they are going, and how much is to be picked up in the new country. I am not pronouncing any judgment upon their conduct, I am merely pointing out the fact. Our Puritan forefathers recked little of property or liberty when these stood in the way of conscience : they defied exile and danger sooner than give up a grain of truth ; but their descendants prefer peace and worldly amusements, and pride themselves on " culture " rather than on heroic faith. The modern believer must have no mysteries, but must have everything planed down to a scientific standard. Abraham " went out, not knowing whither he went," but the moderns must have every information with regard to the way, and then they will not go. If they obey at all, it is because their own superior judgments incline that way : but to go forth, not knowing whither they go, and to go at all hazards, is not to their minds at all. They are 'so highly " cultured " that they prefer to be original, and map out their own way.

Brethren, having once discerned the voice of God, obey without question. If you have to stand alone and nobody will befriend you, stand alone and God will befriend you. If you should get the ill word of those you value most, bear it. What, after all, are ill words, or good words, as compared with the keeping of a clear conscience by walking in the way of the Lord ? The line of truth is narrow as a razor's edge ; and he needs to wear the golden sandals of the peace of God who shall keep to such a line. Through divine grace may we, like Abraham, walk with our hand in the hand of the Lord, even where we cannot see our way !

The obedience which faith produces must be continuous. Having commenced the separated life, Abraham continued to dwell in tents, and sojourn in the land which was far from the place of his birth. His whole life may be thus summed up : " By faith Abraham obeyed." He believed, and, therefore, walked before the Lord in a perfect way. He even offered up his son Isaac. " Abraham's mistake," was it ? Alas for those who dare to talk in that fashion ! " By faith he obeyed," and to the end of his life he was never an original speculator, or inventor of ways for self-will ; but a submissive servant of that great Lord, who deigned to call him " friend." May it be said of everyone here that by faith he obeyed ! Do not cultivate doubt, or you will soon cultivate disobedience. Set this up as your standard, and henceforth be this the epitome of your life—" By faith he obeyed."

III. Just a moment or two upon the third point. Let us consider THE SORT OF LIFE WHICH WILL COME OF THIS FAITH AND OBEDIENCE.

It will be, in the first place, *life without that great risk which else holds us in peril.* A man runs a great risk when he steers himself. Rocks or no rocks, the peril lies in the helmsman. The believer is no longer the helmsman of his own vessel ; he has taken a pilot on board. To believe in God, and to do his bidding, is a great escape from the hazards of personal weakness and folly. If we do as God commands, and do not seem to succeed, it is no fault of ours. Failure itself would be success so long as we did not fail to obey. If we passed through life unrecognized, or were only acknowledged by a sneer from the worldly-wise, and if this were regarded as a failure, it could be borne with equanimity so long as we knew that we had kept our faith towards God, and our obedience to him. Providence is God's business, obedience is ours. What comes out of our life's course must remain with the Lord : to obey is our sole concern. What harvest will come of our sowing we must leave with the Lord of the harvest; but we ourselves must look to the basket and the seed, and scatter our handfuls in the furrows without fail. We can win "Well done, good and *faithful* servant " : to be a successful servant is not in our power, and we shall not be held responsible for it. Our greatest risk is over when we obey. God makes faith and obedience the way of safety.

In the next place, we shall enjoy a *life free from its heaviest cares.* If we were in the midst of the wood, with Stanley, in the centre of Africa, our pressing care would be to find our way out; but when we have nothing to do but to obey, our road is mapped out for us. Jesus says, "Follow me;" and this makes our way plain, and lifts from our shoulders a load of cares. To choose our course by policy is a way of thorns, to obey is as the king's highway. Policy has to tack about, to return upon its own courses, and often to miss the port after all; but faith, like a steam-vessel, steers straight for the harbour's mouth, and leaves a bright track of obedience behind her as she forges ahead. When our only care is to obey, a thousand other cares take their flight. If we sin in order to succeed, we have sown the seeds of care and sorrow, and the reaping will be a grievous one. If we will forsake the path, and try short cuts, we shall have to do a deal of wading through mire and slough, we shall bespatter ourselves from head to foot, we shall be wearied to find our way, and all because we could not trust God, and obey his bidding. Obedience may appear difficult, and it may bring with it sacrifice ; but, after all, it is the nearest and the best road. Her ways are, in the long run, ways of pleasantness, and all her paths are peace. He who, through the Holy Spirit, is always believingly obedient, has chosen the good part. He it is who can sing—

> "I have no cares, ʊ blessèd Lord,
> For all my cares are thine;
> I live in triumph, too, for thou
> Hast made thy triumphs mine."

Or, to change the verse, he is like Bunyan's shepherd-boy in the Valley of Humiliation, for that lowland is part of the great Plain of Obedience, and he also can sing—

> "He that is down need fear no fall,
> He that is low no pride ;
> He that is humble ever shall
> Have God to be his Guide."

Although he may not reach the heights of ambition, nor stand upon the giddy crags of presumption, yet he shall know superior joys. He has hit upon the happiest mode of living under heaven—a mode of life akin to the perfect life above. He shall dwell in God's house, and be still praising him.

The way of obedience is a *life of the highest honour.* Obedience is the glory of a human life—the glory which our Lord has given to his chosen, even his own glory. "He learned obedience." He never struck out an original course, but he did always the things which pleased the Father. Be this our glory. By faith we yield our intelligence to the highest intelligence : we are led, guided, directed ; and we follow where our Lord has gone. To us who believe, he is honour. To a soldier it is the greatest honour to have accomplished his sovereign's command. He does not debase his manhood who subjects it to honourable command ; nay, he is even exalted by obeying in the day of danger. It is no dishonour to have it said :

> " Theirs not to reason why ;
> Theirs but to dare and die."

The bravest and the most honoured of men are those who implicitly obey the command of the King of kings. Among his children, they are best who best know their Father's mind, and yield to it the gladdest obedience. Should we have any other ambition, within the walls of our Father's house, than to be perfectly obedient children before him, and implicitly trustful towards him ?

But, brethren, this is a kind of *life which will bring communion with God.* God often hides his face behind the clouds of dust which his children make by their self-will. If we transgress against him, we shall soon be in trouble ; but a holy walk—the walk described by my text as faith working obedience—is heaven beneath the stars. God comes down to walk with men who obey. If they walk with him, he walks with them. The Lord can only have fellowship with his servants as they obey. Obedience is heaven in us, and it is the preface of our being in heaven. Obedient faith is the way to eternal life—nay, it is eternal life revealing itself.

The obedience of faith creates a form of *life which may be safely copied.* As parents, we wish so to live that our children may copy us to their lasting profit. Teachers should aspire to be what they would have their classes to be. If you go to school to the obedience of faith, you will be good teachers. Children usually exaggerate their models ; but there will be no fear of their going too far in faith, or in obedience to the Lord. I like to hear a man say, when his father has gone, " My dear father was a man that feared God, and I would fain follow him. When I was a boy, I thought him rather stiff and Puritanical ; but now I see he had a good reason for it all. I feel much the same myself, and would do nothing of which God would not approve." The bringing up of families is a very great matter. This is too much neglected nowadays ; and yet it is the most profitable of all holy service, and the hope of the future. Great men, in the best sense, are bred in holy households. God-fearing example at home is the most fruitful of religious agencies. I knew a little humble Dissenting chapel, of the straitest sect of our religion. Culture there was none in the ministry ; but the people were stanch believers. Five or six families, attending that despised ministry, learned to believe what they did believe, and to live upon it. It was by no means a liberal creed which they received, but what they held operated on their lives. Five or six families came out of that place, and became substantial in wealth, and generous in liberality. These all sprang from plain, humble men, who knew their Bibles, and believed the doctrines of grace. They learned to fear God, and to trust in him, and to rest in the old faith, and even in worldly things they prospered

Their descendants, of the third generation, are not all of them of their way of thinking; but they have risen through God's blessing on their grandfathers. These men were fed on substantial meat, and they became sturdy old fellows, able to cope with the world, and fight their way. I would to God that we had more men to-day who would maintain truth at all hazards. Alas! the gutta-percha backbone is common among Dissenters, and they take to politics, and the new philosophy, and therefore we are losing the force of our testimony, and are, I fear, decreasing in numbers too. The Lord give us back those whose examples can be safely copied in all things, even though they be decried as being "rigid" or "too precise"! We serve a jealous God, and a holy Saviour; wherefore let us mind that we do not grieve his Spirit, and cause him to withdraw from us.

Lastly, faith working obedience is a kind of *life which needs great grace*. Every careless professor will not live in this fashion. It will need watchfulness and prayer, and nearness to God, to maintain the faith which obeys in everything. Beloved, "he giveth more grace." The Lord will enable us to add to our faith all the virtues. Whenever you fail in any respect in your lives, do not sit down, and question the goodness of God, and the power of the Holy Ghost; that is not the way to increase the stream of obedience, but to diminish the source of it. Believe more, instead of less. Try, by God's grace, to believe more in the pardon of sin, more in the renovation by the Holy Spirit, more in the everlasting covenant, more in the love that had no beginning, and will never, never cease. Your hope does not lie in rushing into the darkness of doubt; but in returning repentantly into the still clearer light of a steadier faith. May you be helped to do so, and may we, all of us, and the whole multitude of the Lord's redeemed, by faith go on to obey our Lord in all things!

I leave this word with you. Remember, "By faith Abraham obeyed." Have faith in God, and then obey, obey, obey, and keep on obeying, until the Lord shall call you home. Obey on earth, and then you will have learned to obey in heaven. Obedience is the rehearsal of eternal bliss. Practice by obedience now the song which you will sing for ever in glory. God grant his grace to us! Amen.

Obedience Rewarded

" And they departed quickly from the sepulchre with fear and great joy ; and did run to bring his disciples word. And as they went to tell his disciples, behold, Jesus met them, saying, All hail. And they came and held him by the feet, and worshipped him. Then said Jesus unto them, Be not afraid : go tell my brethren that they go into Galilee, and there shall they see me."--Matthew xxviii. 8—10.

THESE holy women, these consecrated Maries, shall be our instructors to-night. They were highly-favoured to be the first witnesses for our risen Lord. Do you wonder why he chose them ? Was it because their hearts were tender, and they were very sad at his death, more sad than the men ? And is it not his wont to come first to those who need him most, and to pour in oil and wine where the wound gapes widest ? It may be so. Was it because they had been the more faithful of the two ; and while some men had denied him, and all had forsaken him, the women were last at Golgotha, as they were now first at the sepulchre ? Did their Lord reward them by dealing with them as they had dealt with him ? That is but his wont. " If ye will walk contrary unto me, then will I also walk contrary unto you," said the Lord to Israel ; and he also said, " I love them that love me ; and those that seek me early shall find me." These holy women did seek their Lord early on the morning of his resurrection, and they found him to a certainty before all others. Was this because Jesus had found the women more spiritual than the apostles ? Certainly, I think that was the case. They had attained the very climax of love, washing his feet with their tears. They had reached the very centre of discipleship ; one of them had chosen the good part, and sat at his feet. Sometimes, where there is less power of understanding, Jesus does give keener powers of perception ; and though Mary Magdalene and the other Mary would never have become Pauls, yet they were of quick eye, like John, and were, therefore, the fittest to see the Saviour in the dawning of the morning, and they were permitted to have the first glimpse of him.

At any rate, be it how it may, they were the first to see their risen

Lord, and we will try to learn something from them to-night. It should be an encouragement to those members of the Church of Christ who are neither pastors nor teachers that, if they live very near to God, they may yet teach pastors and teachers. Get clear views of your Lord, as did these holy women, who had no office in the Church, and yet taught the officers, for they were sent to bear to the apostles the tidings that Jesus Christ had risen from the dead. Not first to them who were the heads of the Church, as it were, but first of all to lowly women, did the Lord appear; and the apostles themselves had to go to school to Mary Magdalene and the other Mary to learn that great truth, "The Lord is risen indeed." We will go to school with the apostles to-night; and may the Lord grant that, while we learn from these holy women, he who taught them may come and teach us! May he who met them meet with us in this house of prayer to-night!

First, I ask you to look at these women *in the way of obedience active.* They ran to bring the disciples word. Secondly, look at them *in the way of obedience rewarded;* for, as they went to tell his disciples, Jesus met them. And then, thirdly, we will go back to the point where we started, and see these women *in the way of obedience refreshed;* for, after they had seen the Lord, they persevered in their heavenly errand, and still went to tell his disciples that he would go before them into Galilee, and that there they should see him.

I. First, then, notice these women IN THE WAY OF OBEDIENCE ACTIVE.

They had gone to the sepulchre to see and also to embalm the body of Christ; but while they were there, an angel appeared to them, and committed to them this charge, "Go quickly, and tell his disciples that he is risen from the dead;" and they went upon their errand with most commendable alacrity. Now, you and I, dear friends, must try to copy them. What thou hast seen, thou must tell; what thou hast been taught, thou must teach. To thee, believer, has been committed the oracle of God. See that thou keep it. Hold it fast, and hold it forth. Thou hast not this light for thyself alone; but that it may shine before men. See thou to this. Peradventure, these women may help thee in so doing.

Observe first, then, that they went about their errand *not doubting the revelation.* The angel said to them, "Tell his disciples that he is risen from the dead; and, behold, he goeth before you into Galilee." They did not stop to ask any question, to make any demur, to utter any critical doubts; but they believed. Now, it is to be thus with you; you cannot be a messenger from God unless you believe. If you do not believe the gospel, do not pretend to preach it. Go home, my dear friends, and bury your head in your doubts, and twist your brains about, and tie them up into knots, and amuse yourself as you like; but do not pretend to go and tell that of which you are not yourself sure. Otherwise, you will lack the accent of confidence, and consequently you will lack the power of persuasion. He that is not firm himself cannot move others. If there be no fulcrum for your lever, where is your power? "I believed; therefore have I spoken," said the psalmist, and he did well; for there must first be the believing, and then the speaking. Leave thou the message to another if thou art not sure of it; let another who *is* sure of it, tell it till thou, too, art sure of it; then mayest thou also run with good tidings from thy Lord. These godly women leaped at once into the full conviction that Christ was risen, and therefore they hastened to tell the tidings to the disciples.

And, again, they obeyed, *not discussing their authority* to go and proclaim this news. What avails it if I believe the truth, and yet am not empowered to teach it? According to some, I can only be authorized by some special ceremonial; I must undergo certain processes before I may be permitted to preach; but the angel said to these women, "Go and tell," and they went to tell. They did not hesitate, they asked no question about apostolical succession, or episcopal ordination, or anything of the kind. They were told to go, and they went. Hast thou heard Jesus speak to thee? Dost thou know his love? Hast thou an inward persuasion that thou hast to tell thy friends what great things he has done for thee? Then, go in this thy might. If thou hast any hesitancy about thy right to labour for thy Lord, if thou doubtest that passage, "Let him that heareth say, Come," then go not; for, if thou dost not believe that thou hast a right to go, thy going will be with an inward weakness, and thou wilt be taken up rather with thyself than with thy message, and with the heart of him to whom thou carriest it. I love to hear men say that they *must* do this and that, for only that which is done under the imperious necessity of a divine impulse will ever be followed by any great result. If thou canst live without preaching the gospel, do live without preaching it; for if God has sent thee, thou wilt say with Paul, "Woe is unto me, if I preach not the gospel!" And thou, my sister, if thou art sent to do any work for God, and hast a yearning to win souls, thou hast a fire in thy bones which cannot be restrained; thou couldst no more be stayed from speaking of Jesus than the sun can be stayed from shining in mid heaven. May God grant that we may have among us many who, in going forth to work for Christ, are sure about what they have to tell; and sure about their authority to tell it!

This being so with these women, we notice, next, that they went on their errand *not declining on account of weakness.* They might have said, "Oh, we are not the people to go to the apostles!" Mary Magdalene might have said, "You know what I used to be; would you have me go and talk to John, and James, and Peter?" Indeed, the holy women might at once have refused the commission, and said, "We do not feel ourselves qualified; we have a natural timidity and modesty which put it out of the question that we should go on such a service as this." But not a word of that kind did they utter; and dear brethren and sisters, while souls are dying, dare we hesitate on account of weakness? Do you not think that it is the man who is most conscious of weakness who is usually the chosen man for the Lord's service? Did not Moses wish to decline the office of leader of Israel because he was slow of speech? Did not Isaiah cry, "Woe is me! for I am undone; because I am a man of unclean lips"? And if you are conscious of weakness as great as that of these godly women, or greater even than theirs, yet still I say that the pressure of human necessity, and the pressure of the divine message, should be so heavy upon you that you should say, "I will go even as did the lepers of old, when they had found out the plenty that there was in the camp of the Syrians, and knew of the sore famine in Samaria." They could not sit still; but, all over leprosy as they were, they must go to the king's household, and tell them that there was bread enough and to spare, and that the people need not die of hunger. Oh, yes, we must go; even we must go! The time may have been when only the choice and pick of the Church were needed for holy service, but these times are not now. When sin abounds, when error rages, when the faithful are but few, then every man, and every woman, and even every babe in grace, must speak, or lisp, or prattle the good news that Christ is risen from the dead, and is able to save and bless.

Then, dear friends, as these women were not detained from this work by a sense of weakness, so they obeyed, *not held back by curiosity*. They might have stayed to look at the sepulchre. They were invited to come and see the place where the Lord lay; and, like the two disciples, they might have gone in, and observed how the napkin was laid by itself, and the linen cloths were folded. I think that, if you and I had had the opportunity of looking into that wonderful sepulchre where the Lord lay, we should have liked to linger there all through that day, to worship and adore. But no curiosity, nay, no devotion, kept them at the sepulchre when they once had the command to go and tell the disciples that Christ was risen from the dead. Now, these days are full of temptation. We have a thousand fields for curiosity to wander in. How shall we settle this debate? How shall we answer that criticism? Every day brings to light some fresh objection, some new theory. Shall we stop till we have answered every objection, till we have destroyed every theory? No, my brethren, we cannot afford to stop. Let others debate; we must declare. Let others discuss; we must proclaim that Jesus Christ has come into the world to save sinners. Sinners, look you to him; and, looking, you shall live. We must make this the burden of our daily conversation, the constant theme of our talk,—"Christ Jesus came into the world to save sinners, even the very chief of them." We must keep to this. As these women were not turned aside to make any curious observation, so must not we be; but we must keep to our one work of telling his disciples where to look for him, and bidding them follow him.

And, dear friends, again, I want you to notice that they were *not hampered by their emotions*. It is a very blessed thing sometimes to have an opportunity of indulging your emotions. These women were subject to the influences of two opposite currents, "fear and great joy." Fear put wings to their heels; and great joy seemed to lend them extra speed. By the two together they ran to bring the disciples word. It may be very pleasant to get alone, and spend much time in close communion with Christ; the more of it the better. It may be well to practise introspection until you see the evil of your heart, and are filled with fear. It may be well to look up, and see the beauties of your Lord, and the glories of his Advent, till you are filled with great joy. But neither of these must be allowed to keep you away from actual service, and the continual telling out of the gospel of

Christ. I have known it to be the case. I remember a good man, who was a great authority on the Book of the Revelation. I am sorry to say that, great as he was on the Revelation, his influence was very bad on his children at home. He knew all about the seven trumpets, but he did not know much about the seven boys and girls he had at home; so they grew up very badly. Never break the balance of holy emotions and sacred duties; let us have our fear and our great joy; but, at the same time, we must not sit down because we have great joy, but we must run on the Lord's errand, joy and all. Let us run as fast as we can, whether we fear or whether we rejoice. Learn that lesson from these godly women. You feel very dull ; go to your Bible-class. You feel as if you had done no good for a long time ; go on in the Lord's work. But God has greatly blessed you, and you are getting rather old, and you want rest; go on with your work, run to bring the disciples word whether you feel fear or joy. Stand you over your work, be *in-stant*—standing over it, in season and out of season, constant and instant in the service of your blessed Lord and Master. If you are not, these holy women will put you to shame, and I must send you to this dames' school, old as you are, to learn a little lesson from these godly dames as to how you ought to serve God.

Once more, notwithstanding all that might have been said to make their footsteps slow, we find that they were *not hindered by propriety or indifference*. They travelled to their work as quickly as they could : "and did run to bring his disciples word." Now, one hardly likes to think of Mary Magdalene and that other Mary running. My good sisters here are many of them very diligent in their service, but they do not forget that there is a kind of reputable pace for ladies ; yet these holy women ran. They will get out of breath by running! Never mind; never mind. "They did run to bring the disciples word." We are great slaves to propriety, are we not, the most of us ? The other day, a brother called out in the middle of a sermon ; and on another morning, a sister exclaimed while I was preaching ; and some of you thought that it was very improper, did you not? Well, I suppose that it was, but I was very glad of it; and I did not see the slightest objection to the impropriety when I felt that the truth that was being preached was enough to make the stones speak. Why should not those persons cry out ? When you are about the Lord's work, you know that it is well to be very quiet and calm, and take things steadily. That is well; but sometimes we can do better than well. We have the steam up, and we cannot help it, and we have to go ahead, and we must go. Thus these godly women were running along. They will put their garments out of shape ; they will spoil the look of their faces! I do not know what will not happen ; but they do not care about that. "They did run to bring the disciples word." How often have I seen it, in the country, when somebody has stepped into a cottage ; perhaps it has been the minister, or some dear Christian friend, and the good woman has said, "I must run and fetch in my neighbour," and she has rushed out of the door, and down the front garden, and across the street, and she has brought her sister or her friend to come and hear the good word, and she has never thought that it was at all improper for her to do it. Dear friend, in the service of God, impropriety is often piety. It was said that Mr. Rowland Hill "rode upon the back of Order and Decorum." "Well," said he, "I will try to make that true," so he called his two horses Order and Decorum; and thus, if he did not ride on their backs, he made them pull him to and from Surrey Chapel. Order and decorum are hardly worth more than to be used as horses. They are very respectable animals; but sometimes disorder and the want of decorum may be predicated of an earnest, zealous heart, and may be very much to the credit of that heart. "They did run to bring his disciples word." Brethren and sisters, some of us ought to run, for we have not much time. We are getting grey, years are telling upon us; so let us run. We may not have many more opportunities; we may be kept to our bed, or tied to the house; let us run while we can. Sometimes we are warned not to do too much: let us try to do too much; let us be indiscreetly loving to our Lord, let us run to bring the disciples word, even at the cost of putting ourselves out of breath.

I think that we have now learned all that we need to learn from these good women about their being in the way of obedience, that is to say, if we *have* learned it; but have we learned it? Are all of you Christian people who are here to-night running on your Master's errands? Have all of you received a commission from Christ? Have you all had a message from him? Are you carrying it? Some of you are strangers here this evening. Let me beg you not to live a single week without having something to do for your Lord, knowing what it is, and getting to it in the spirit of these holy women.

II. But now, secondly, observe these holy women IN THE WAY OF OBEDIENCE REWARDED.

First, they were rewarded by *a most delightful visitation:* "As they went to tell his disciples, behold, Jesus met them." He has ways of meeting his disciples now, in the power of his Spirit, manifesting himself to them. There are some of his disciples who never get these visitations, and I think that it is because they are not running to bring his disciples word. Nobody fidgets a busy person like an idle body. Have you never had a servant doing some work for you, and crawling about in such a way that you could hardly bear yourself? Well now, the Lord Jesus Christ does not feel at home with lazy Christians; and I believe that he reserves his fellowship for the sufferers and the workers. When you are in the way of service, he will meet you. So you have not seen his face for a long time? Have you a class in the Sabbath-school? Are you a tract-distributor? Are you a preacher in the villages? "No, dear sir, I do nothing of the sort." Well, then, I do not think that you will meet him just yet; but I think that, if you had a call to some of these good works, and you obeyed it, it is highly probable that you would then say, "Being in the way, the Lord met with me." Oh, yes, when you have love, and joy, and light in your heart, it will often happen that, while you are talking about Christ to others, you will have a blessing come to your own soul! Many times has it occurred to the preacher that, if he has not edified anybody else, he has preached himself into a right state of heart, and he is sure that he has had one hearer who was the better for the sermon. Beloved Christian brothers and sisters, especially sisters, for the text, you see, comes from the sisters, and ought to go back to the sisters, get into the path of duty if you would win this reward of a delightful visitation. You sometimes sing,—

" When wilt thou come unto me, Lord ? "

You can answer your own prayer, to a large extent, by running upon your Lord's errands.

The next reward these women received was *a very cheering salutation :* "Jesus met them, saying, All hail." I do not know whether it was in the Hebrew that he spoke; if so, I suppose that he uttered the usual salutation, "Peace be unto you!" As we get it in the Greek, one is inclined to think that he used the Greek language, and spoke the word which signifies, "Rejoice! Joy be unto you!" Our translators very properly thought that the best thing they could do was to give you the old Saxon expression, "All hail! Health be to you! May you be in good health, may you be hale!" "All hail!" You know that we use the expression, "Hail fellow, well met!" Well, that indicates great sociability; and hence you can see the wrong of a Christian saying it to an ungodly man; but Christ comes to his people, and says, "All hail!" I often wonder that he ever used that word, since by it he was betrayed when the traitor said, "Hail, Master!" But yet it was his mother's word. Did not the angel Gabriel say to Mary, "Hail, thou that art highly favoured, the Lord is with thee : blessed art thou among women"? And he used it here, "All hail!" Well, when Jesus Christ comes to us with words of such endearment, such brotherhood, it ought to make us glad.

Last Tuesday night, I saw a brother who, I trust, has just been converted to God. He may be here to-night; if so, he must excuse my telling you this. He cannot read well; but he is teaching himself to read, and he said to me something that touched me very much. He said, "Do you know, I read this week the most wonderful thing I ever heard of; I dare say you know all about it, sir; but it was a very wonderful thing to me"? I asked, "What was it?" "Well," he replied, "you know, I was spelling it over, and I found that Christ said, 'I call you not servants; but I have called you friends.' That knocked me over," he said, "*me* a friend of *his*, me a friend of his? And he calls me so. I was obliged to think that I must have made a mistake, and I had to read it over to see if it could be so, that he really called me a friend. And further down he said, 'These things have I spoken unto you, that ye should not be offended.' There, I thought, what difference would it make to him if I were offended? And to think of my being offended with him! It is much more likely that he will be offended with me. It is very wonderful." That is a most blessed way of reading the Bible for the first time, to see these wonders as they break upon you. Well, now, it is just as my friend found it to be; the Lord does come to us with very sweet familiarity, he uses what the French call "tutoyage." In speaking to us, he utters the familiar " thee " and " thou "; and he sits down to eat in company with us, calls us to his table, and there bids us eat and drink with him. It is wonderful, as my friend said; but it is thus that Jesus deals with those who love and serve him. And what a reward it is for the Lord's servants when he says to them, "All hail! I am your Companion; I have done well to meet you; I am glad to see you. All health be to you! Every blessing rest upon you!" Something more than "Salem", the "peace" of the old Covenant, is this "All hail!" of the new Covenant, of which the Incarnate God is the great Expositor. That was the cheering salutation with which the risen Saviour rewarded the obedience of these godly women.

They had also *an assuring satisfaction* as another reward of their obedience, for they were permitted to prove that their Lord was really risen from the dead. Before Thomas had done it, they did it. "They came and held him by the feet." He was no spectre, no phantom; it was no dream that deceived them. Christ was really risen; there he stood in solid flesh and blood, and they held him by the feet. I believe that, when we are at work for the Lord with all our heart, he sometimes enables us to get grips of truth that we do not have at other times, and we lay hold on it with unrelaxing grasp. People talk about "honest doubt"; and ask me to doubt. I cannot doubt; I live in the enjoyment of the eternal facts. I could sooner doubt my own existence than doubt the doctrines of Christ, they have become such substantial verities to me; I have tasted and handled them; I cannot have a doubt about them. It was so with these godly women, they knew that Christ was risen, for they came and held him by the feet.

But, at the same time, they had, mixed with this experience, *a rapturous adoration*. "They held him by the feet, and worshipped him." It is of no use to be persuaded of a doctrine,—that is, mentally to hold it,—unless there is the spirit of worship going with it, so that you adore your Lord while you hold to him and his truth. These women not merely felt that Jesus was there as a man, but they knew that he was also God, they were sure of it, and therefore they worshipped him. It takes a lot of faith, while you are holding a man, to worship him at the same time, because your grip of the human body is a proof of its materialism, and you say to yourself, "This is a man," and therefore you do not worship him; but these women knew that Jesus was God as well as man, so they could mingle the holding by his feet with the worship due to his Godhead. In a natural sense, none of us can exactly imitate these worshipping women; but those who are taught of God the Holy Ghost, and who know how to be familiar and yet to be devout, will draw near to Christ, and hold him by the feet, and at the same time, worship him with solemn awe and sacred joy.

Now, this is the reward that I want my dear friends here to have. I know that the most of you have some work on hand for the Master; if you are getting at all dull and heavy, I beg you not to give it up. Stick to it; but pray the Lord to meet with you. May he meet you here to-night! If not, may he meet you on the way home, or in your bed-chamber! Nothing is so sweet as the sight of our Lord risen from the dead, to know that he lives, and that we also shall live because he lives, and to get a sight of him as alive, and living for us. This puts nerve into us, and sends us back to our service greatly refreshed. That is to be my last point, and upon it I will speak very briefly.

III. Thirdly, notice these holy women IN THE WAY OF OBEDIENCE REFRESHED, for, having seen and touched their Lord, they were now sent away to his brethren.

Before they went forth the second time, *they were perfectly calm, and happy in the Lord.* I think that it is almost essential to any great success in serving the Lord that we should be on the best of terms with him, and not be fluttered, frightened, worried, perturbed, questioning. Having worshipped, and held him, and heard him say, " All hail," you will then feel that, by the power of his love and the authority of his divinity, he sends you forth as his messenger.

Notice, next, that the angel said to the women, " Go quickly, and tell his disciples "; but Jesus said, " Go tell my brethren." Thus, *their commission was sweetened.* And if it be with you as it was with them, you will get to be more tender in the delivery of your message. You will begin to feel nearer of kin to those to whom you speak ; you will perceive more of the love of Christ to them. You will not merely be talking in your Sunday-school class to " boys and girls out of the street ", you will feel that you are speaking to those of whom Jesus said, " Suffer the little children to come unto me." I shall not be preaching to mere " men and women of our fallen race ", but to those in whom I hope to find the brethren of my Lord. In seeking to do good, there is nothing like the plan of getting close to the people. Up in Scotland, I have often seen the fishermen standing right in the middle of the river ; that is a good place to fish ; it is better than being on the bank. Get among the fish, and you will catch them. Get to feel your relationship to the soul you deal with, and your Lord's relationship to him, and you will preach or teach much better than you have ever done in the past. Thus these women went with their commission sweetened by their Lord's loving words, " Go tell *my brethren.*"

Notice, again, that *their confidence in their message was increased.* They believed it when the angel uttered it ; but they believed it still more emphatically when their Master repeated it to them. Besides, his telling it to them was the best proof that it was true. He could not have told them that he was risen from the dead, if he had not been risen from the dead. So truth, when it comes to us in Christ, is its own proof. You may doubt it while it is simply preached by men ; but you surely will never doubt it when Jesus himself, in his own person, comes to you, and says himself, " This is the truth ; open your heart and soul, and receive it." May the Lord do this for many here !

And then, *these women went on their way with increased joy.* They had no great fear, nay, not even a little fear, for their great joy had swallowed up their fear. I should have liked to have seen them go in among the apostles, exclaiming, " The Lord is risen indeed." They might say, " But Mary, we saw you last night looking as miserable as possible." " Ah ! " she would answer, " but Christ is risen. I have seen him, and he said to me, ' Be not afraid,' and I am not afraid either of the Jews or of anybody else, for he is risen. He said to me, ' All hail,' and it is all hail ; all is well, for the Lord is risen." Testifying of their Lord in this spirit, they expected to be believed, and they were believed. May the Lord put you also into such a condition to-night, that you may say, " I know now more than I ever did before the truth of my Lord's gospel, and I will tell it as though I could not think that anybody would doubt it. I will tell it expecting that they must believe it; " and they will believe it, for according to your faith so shall it be unto you.

As for you, my dear hearers, who do not know my Lord, how I wish that you did! He is a living Christ; he is no lifeless picture on the walls, not a dead character in a book. He is the living Lord. He has come to us, and given us eternal life; and if you come to him, he will in no wise cast you out. If you only look to him, you shall live. If you take his yoke upon you, and learn of him, you shall find rest unto your souls. I would that you might do so this very night; may the Lord bless you in so doing!

Thus I have preached to you, and now there are some believers to be baptized. That is the second part of our work. At the end of this chapter we read, " Go ye therefore, and teach all nations, baptizing them in the name of the Father, and of the Son, and of the Holy Ghost: teaching them to observe all things whatsoever I have commanded you." We will at another time go on with the teaching that follows this evening's meditation, if the Lord will.